The
SEVENTH-
DAY
OX

Other books by Bradley Booth:

Dare to Stand Alone
Escape from Egypt
Esther
Noah: Chosen One
Noah: The End of the World
Plagues in the Palace
Prince of Dreams
The Prodigal
Shepherd Warrior
They Call Him the Miracle Man
Time Warp

To order, call 1-800-765-6955.

Visit us at **www.reviewandherald.com** for information on other Review and Herald® products.

The SEVENTH-DAY OX

And Other Miracle Stories From Russia

Bradley Booth

REVIEW AND HERALD® PUBLISHING ASSOCIATION
Since 1861 | www.reviewandherald.com

This book was
Edited by Kalie Kelch
Cover designed by Trent Truman
Interior designed by Tina M. Ivany
Cover photos by Cover art by © istockphoto.com / claudiodivizia / Rouzes / zoomstudio; © 123rf.com / James Steidl

Typeset: Bembo 11/14

PRINTED IN U.S.A.

15   14   13   12   11   5   4   3   2

Library of Congress Cataloging-in-Publication Data

Booth, Bradley, 1957-
  The seventh-day ox, and other miracle stories from Russia / Bradley Booth.
    p. cm.
1. Seventh-Day Adventists—Soviet Union. 2. Animals—Religious aspects—Seventh-Day Adventists. 3. Miracles—Soviet Union. I. Title.
  BX6153.4.S65B66 2011
  286.7'47—dc22

                                        2010011258

ISBN 978-0-8280-2517-1

DEDICATION

This book is dedicated to the faithful Christians in Russia who have sacrificed so much to spread the gospel and to the animals of God's creation that helped them do it.

CONTENTS

THE SEVENTH-DAY OX

CHAPTER 1

Nickolai Panchuk stared at the four walls of the jail cell around him. The cold gray concrete made him feel trapped as though he were in a tomb—cold and frightened and alone.

What would become of him? What was to be his fate? He had refused to cooperate with the KGB thus far—refused to betray the whereabouts of yet another fledgling church he had helped organize only a month ago. It wasn't a large church—just a company of believers in the city of Kiev, the capital of the Ukraine—but Nickolai had refused to turn over a list of the members to the KGB.

And who could blame him? The gospel message was spreading so fast that every few months, now, Nickolai was forming yet another company of believers. At present he was shepherd and pastor of eleven such congregations.

Groups typically met to worship in houses and cellars and barns, but 15 or 20 members seemed to be the magic number before the group was considered too large. The places they met were just too small to hold more than that number. Then too, everyone loved the close-knit family feeling they experienced from being part of a company of Seventh-day Adventist Christians.

Nickolai leaned back against the cold wall of the prison cell and closed his eyes. The peace that came from worshiping with like believers was more than enough pay for the pain and hardship he had faced during the last few months. It wasn't easy, but he was getting used to it. Five times now the KGB had cornered him to find out information about the Seventh-day Adventist Church members who were meeting in scattered companies in the towns and small villages of the area. Twice they had come to his house, and three times they had used a public confrontation to humiliate him and try to make him talk.

The KGB needed that crucial list of church members—without it everything was a hit-and-miss operation for them—like sifting for needles in the chaff of a haystack.

Fortunately for Nickolai, the KGB in the area where he lived were decent enough to leave his family out of it. Other pastors in Russia had not been so lucky. Nickolai had heard terrible stories of what the KGB sometimes did to get pastors to talk.

But Nickolai always remained steadfast and determined in his promise to leave everything in God's hands. His faith was strong. He would not betray the church members and their trust no matter what the cost to himself or his family.

But this time the interrogation process was different—it was obvious the KGB had something else in mind for Nickolai. When he had first arrived at the KGB headquarters, they had sat him in a chair and kept him awake for more than two days. They had used the proverbial bright lights in his eyes, shouting tactics, and even threats of where they might send him to help straighten him out.

But all to no avail. Nickolai had remained undaunted and unmovable. Their tactics did not intimidate him. Unfortunately, the KGB were more than persistent. They were determined! What was to come next was anybody's guess, though Nickolai felt it didn't take a rocket scientist to figure it out.

He was considered an enemy of the state. Christians were high on the list of rebels who needed to be reformed and retooled for society. If they could be punished enough, maybe they would finally see the light. Those were the words from the top on down, but Nickolai guessed that few in the upper ranks of the military ever bothered themselves about what actually happened to pastors like Nickolai. As long as the KGB methods produced results, they cared little about the details.

Nickolai wondered what time it was. He had no watch, and the scant meals they brought him were the only indications that time was passing, though he was sure he had been in his cell for several days now. For Nickolai, time seemed to stand still.

Suddenly Nickolai heard footsteps coming down the long concrete corridor. The footsteps slowed and then stopped in front of his cell, and he could hear a hand fumbling with a key in the door. "On your feet!" a voice barked.

Nickolai scrambled to his feet in time to see a big burly figure fill the doorway. A lone 40-watt bulb burning in the corridor cast eerie shadows past the hulking frame. Nickolai assumed that the man was one of the guards who had been bringing him his meals since he had arrived.

"The Boss wants to see you!"

Nickolai waited for the guard to give him specific orders, but the big man simply pulled him into the corridor and pushed him in the direction he wanted him to go.

They went up a flight of concrete stairs, and then down another hallway until they came to a big room with a large desk in it and two straight-backed chairs. Other than that, the only thing in the room was another lightbulb burning feebly high overhead.

Behind the desk sat an intimidating officer in a gray-green uniform—a manila folder lay open on the desk in front of him. He never bothered to raise his eyes when Nickolai walked in, but continued staring at the contents of the folder over horn-rimmed reading glasses. A shot glass and bottle of vodka sat on the desk beside him, and a long cigarette dangled from his clean-shaven mouth.

Nickolai remained standing, not daring to sit down in the second chair. Whatever was coming next would no doubt be better received standing up.

"Preacher man!" The officer threw out the expression he had been using on Nickolai for the past several days. "Have you given my proposition some more thought?" The officer still did not look Nickolai in the eye, and Nickolai was grateful for it. Eye contact was a code of intimidation with the KGB. If a prisoner should respond to such a gesture with eye contact of his own, it was understood that the victim was ready to finally come to some kind of agreement.

And for Nickolai, that was impossible. He knew he could never bring himself to agree to the KGB's terms that he reveal the list of the church members in his district! Never! Never in a thousand years!

But the officer was waiting, and Nickolai knew there was nothing for him to do except tell the "Boss" exactly what he had told him before.

His mind was made up—there would be no compromise, no "deal." For Nickolai there was no other choice, and he knew the officer would soon grow impatient because of it.

"I'm sorry, sir, but I can't comply. My God and my conscience won't allow it."

The officer pushed Nickolai's folder away and folded his arms across his chest. Nickolai kept his eyes fixed on the wall behind the officer's head, but he could tell that the man was staring at him over the tops of his glasses, and it made him nervous.

CHAPTER 2

Is that all you have to say for yourself!" The KGB officer growled. Nickolai hesitated for only a moment. "Sir! That is my final decision."

The officer shook his head. "You're serious aren't you?" He took the cigarette from his mouth and tapped a long string of ashes onto the floor.

"I am, sir."

"You are a stubborn man." The officer shook his head again and sighed in frustration. "We've used all the usual methods and forms of diplomacy we know." He put the cigarette back into his mouth and took another long drag from it. "I wish you were on our side, preacher man. It would make my job so much easier."

Preacher Man. Nickolai dared to smile at the nickname the officer had given him. And *diplomacy*? Their process of interrogation was anything but diplomatic. Victims of the KGB had choices alright, but they were very one-sided. Either allow yourself to be persuaded and comply, or else pay the piper.

The officer finished his cigarette and poured a shot glass of vodka. Surprisingly he extended the glass in Nickolai's direction, but Nickolai declined with a simple, "Thank you, sir, but I don't drink."

The officer grunted and set the glass down roughly, spilling half of the vodka on the file folder in front of him. His mood quickly turned from warm to sour.

"Well, I can see that I'm getting nowhere fast, preacher man. I've got more important things to do than waste my time here with you!" he raised his voice. "I might as well be talking to the wall for all the good this conversation is doing!

"We've kept you awake, hammering at you incessantly, but you won't break! We've offered you bribes and positions in our organization! We've even been willing to concede some of the restrictions we've put on you during past encounters, but you always give us the same answer! It's obvious you're going to be of no help here!"

The officer raised a hand to shake his finger at Nickolai. "I'm tired of this nonsense! We were hoping to talk to you and make some sense out of this whole situation, but I can see that you are more stubborn than ever."

He pulled a handkerchief from his uniform pocket and sopped up the spilled vodka before closing the manila folder. "Your case is out of my hands. My superiors expect results, and if I can't get them, then there's going to be a price to pay."

His voice grew calm again. "I like you Nickolai, but if we can't come to an agreement, there is nothing I can do to save you." It was the first time he had used Nickolai's name since Nickolai had first come to the prison five days before.

"I've been instructed to inform you that you are being sentenced to labor in a prison camp in Siberia. Unless you are ready to answer our questions, there is nothing more I can do."

To Nickolai's surprise, the officer stood to his feet and extended his hand. "Good luck, preacher man. May your God be with you." He gestured toward the door, nodded to the guard, and then sat down again to finish his paperwork.

As Nickolai turned to go, he thought he saw a look of pity in the KGB officer's eyes, but he knew he must be mistaken. KGB officers were known for their hard hearts and their unflinching determination to get information out of their victims.

Nickolai was led back to his cell. As the door clanged shut behind him, he took stock of his situation. Things were not looking good. There was no doubt that he had made the right decision, but at what cost? He had no idea how long he would be sentenced to the frigid wastelands of Siberia. Years? Decades? Until he died?

He cringed as he thought of the dreaded sentence so frightening to any prisoner's ears—banishment to the Siberian frontier. Summer temperatures in Siberia could be cool and damp, with swarms of black flies and huge, bloodthirsty mosquitoes everywhere. And with no towns or settlements in that vast wasteland, he had heard that escape was impossible. There was little chance of survival should a prisoner even attempt to make an escape.

But it was the winters in Siberia that were the most fearsome for a prisoner. Temperatures sometimes dropped to 50 degrees below zero, and with the biting wind that chased its way across the northland, living conditions were unthinkable.

Nickolai shivered in his cell just thinking about the prospects of such a future. There was still time for him to rethink the whole thing, time to change his mind and escape the fate he had been handed.

But of course Nickolai knew that he would never do that. He could not. It was against everything he had ever believed in and stood for all his life. Allegiance to the Higher Power in his life was the most important thing now. The Russian KGB could take away his pulpit. They could take away his freedom and even his health, but they would never take away his choice to serve God and be true to Him.

And now at the recommendation of the secret police, the communist government was going to exile him to an outpost prison in Siberia. It was a heavy price to pay, but Nickolai had no doubt in his mind that God was going to be with him.

He would not give up his resolve to guard his church member's names. He would continue to speak for God no matter where he lived. He would witness for God no matter what it cost him.

And who knew? Maybe the Holy Spirit would use him to do even greater things for God than he was already doing. Time would tell.

CHAPTER 3

Nickolai awoke with a start as he felt the engineer apply the air breaks to the line of train cars. The sun was not yet up, but streaks of magenta were creasing the horizon as Nickolai sleepily stared out the train car windows. Just a few hours before, the gentle swaying of the train had lulled him into a fitful sleep. Handcuffed to the seat, it had been difficult to stretch out in a comfortable position.

He sat up stiffly and noticed that most of the other passengers were still sleeping. Some were stretched out on upper bunks, some across the lower seats as he was, while still others were sprawled in the aisles on the floor.

The previous afternoon two army soldiers had boarded the train with Nickolai and two other prisoners and set out for the city of Omsk. They knew little as to the details of their journey, except that they would eventually end up at a Siberian prison camp.

Nickolai tried to remain positive in spite of his uncomfortable surroundings, which included being handcuffed at all times, except for when he needed to use the bathroom—but even then, a guard stood outside the door. It wasn't much, but Nickolai was grateful for the small bag of bread and can of water the prisoners received each day. The rations were meager, but as the train chugged eastward along the tracks, Nickolai's mind kept returning to a familiar verse in Scripture: "Even your bread and water shall be sure." The words to the text comforted him when he thought about the literal fulfillment of that promise.

The trip was tedious, but Nickolai knew that even on this train he should be ready to speak for God and witness for his faith. Somewhere during that first morning on the train, Nickolai struck up a conversation with a middle-aged man sitting next to him. The man's face looked drawn and tired even after a night's rest. When Nickolai expressed care and concern, the man introduced himself as Yuri and said that he was returning to his home in the small town of Krasnodon. He worked in the city of Kharkov, but his wife and children lived in Krasnodon, tending to the gardens at the family dacha. It was difficult for the family to be apart all the time, but like most families in the Ukraine, it was the only way they could make ends meet financially.

Yuri had recently received a letter from home telling him that his wife was sick and that he'd better catch the next train to Krasnodon. "She has bleeding spells, usually from the nose," Yuri confided. "The doctors have done all they can, but it is not a good situation. One time last year she bled so much that she had to stay in bed for more than a week until she could get her strength back."

He paused and then continued, "Her condition is very serious again, but we don't know what's causing the bleeding or how to stop it. I'm afraid I'm going to lose her, and it scares me more than anything I've ever had to face in my life."

The man's voice grew somber. "It frightens her, too," he added, and Nickolai could see fear clearly written on his face. "Death is a dark place—no one knows what happens to a person when they die."

Nickolai listened to the man and saw the desperate need in his eyes. He could tell that this man was in need of comfort. If Nickolai could give him even one ray of hope, he knew it would help.

And so, Nickolai began to tell him stories about Jesus and the healing power that God can bring to a life. He explained to Yuri that he didn't need to worry about death, because the Creator of life had conquered death. Jesus, God's Son, had died for the sins of the world and then rose again from the dead. He is in heaven now and has the power to give the gift of eternal life to all who will accept it.

"Are you a priest?" Yuri suddenly asked. "You speak of God as though you know him well, and you speak of the future as though you have already seen it."

Nickolai smiled warmly. "I'm a pastor," he admitted, "and I love God very much. As for the future, I have a wonderful book that tells me what to expect so that I can be ready for it when it comes."

"I wish it was possible for you to come to my village," Yuri said. "My wife would be so happy to meet you, I'm sure. Maybe you could even help her with her illness."

It was then that Nickolai shared with Yuri and the others passengers why he was on the train as a prisoner. He spoke about his churches and how much everyone loved Jesus. He spoke of his refusal to give the KGB the names of all his members.

No one said anything as Nickolai told his story. By the looks on their faces, he could tell that many of the passengers sympathized with him in his plight and the injustice of his sentence. Of course, no one dared express their true feelings for fear that they might be accused of being sympathizers and end up being sent to a prison camp as Nickolai was.

Yuri bowed his head dejectedly when he understood that Nickolai was not going to be able to go to his house and pray for his wife as he wished. However, what he said next surprised even Nickolai.

"Would you be willing to pray for my wife right now?" he asked.

Tears came to Nickolai's eyes as he witnessed the measure of faith Yuri had gained in the few minutes they had been talking.

The train car grew silent as Nickolai bowed his head and prayed for Yuri's sick wife and his children. It seemed that heaven had drawn very close, and the Spirit of God was hovering near.

When Nickolai finished praying, he noticed that a solemn look had come to the faces of many passengers on board. It was as if they understood the pain Yuri must be going through, but it also appeared as though Nickolai's prayer had touched them personally, too.

When the train approached Krasnodon later that afternoon, Yuri thanked Nickolai for the prayer he had offered for his wife and family. And he expressed disappointment that he would never see Nickolai again.

"Take heart," Nickolai challenged Yuri. "We will meet each other again in heaven one day."

At this announcement several of the other passengers began to listen again, and some even came to sit close to where Nickolai and Yuri were talking.

"Because Jesus loves us so much, He left us some very special words. He doesn't want us to be discouraged while we wait for Him to come and take us home with Him.

"'Let not your heart be troubled,'" Nickolai began, "'you believe in God, believe also in Me. In My Father's house are many rooms. If it were not so I would have told you. I go to prepare a place for you, and if I go to prepare a place for you, I will come again and receive you unto myself that where I am, there you may be also.'"

As the train pulled into the station, Nickolai prayed once again for Yuri's wife and children, and then for each person in that small circle on the train. Again Nickolai called upon the Master Physician to do for Yuri's wife what the doctors could not do, and again he sensed the Holy Spirit drawing near. It was an awesome and inspiring experience.

There were many tears when Nickolai finished his prayer, and many handshakes and hugs. It was as if Nickolai were a Christian apostle saying goodbye to his faithful members on one of his missionary trips around the world.

CHAPTER 4

During the next few days on the train, Nickolai brought many more people to God. Several gave their hearts to Jesus and became Christians. Nickolai could not baptize them, but he encouraged them to find an Adventist pastor and ask that this be done for them.

After the train had been traveling eastward for several days, it finally neared the city of Omsk. Nickolai had heard that the prisoners would be transferred to another train when they arrived in Omsk, but that was as much information as he could get. No one had told him yet how far they had to go or how long it was going to take for the entire trip. Judging by the distance to the port on the North Sea and the speed of the slowly moving train, Nickolai was guessing the trip would span at least ten days.

Near sunset of the sixth day, the train arrived in Omsk, a city known for its industry and oil production. Within the hour Nickolai and the other prisoners were transferred to a train heading north. By dark the train was lumbering across the plains toward the North Sea, and Nickolai had settled in again for the remainder of the trip.

There were almost no passengers on this leg of the journey because they were now riding on a freight train. In fact, other than the three prisoners and the two soldiers guarding them, the only other riders were the engineer, his furnace stoker, and a half dozen other workers who took up their positions near the end of the train.

Nickolai and his two fellow prisoners were confined in a mail car. Heavy manacles were now attached to their legs as well as their wrists so that they wouldn't be able to escape. Nickolai smiled to himself as he stared out the window of the mail car and watched the landscape pass slowly by. Even if he could escape in these wastelands, where would he go?

As the train wound its way northward, the country became even more flat and littered with swampy muskegs. By now there were no trees in the desolate terrain.

For three long days the train crawled northward across mosquito infested tundra and around small boggy lakes, but only once or twice did Nickolai see even a small village. He did catch a glimpse of reindeer herds, and now and then a few hunters following the herds. What would it be like to be on the open tundra, Nickolai wondered? Would he be free to come and go as he pleased at the prison, or would he be locked up most of the time? It was at these moments that Nickolai found himself wondering about the decisions he had made during the past few weeks.

But then he remembered his commission. He was a pastor for God and an evangelist to the world. If God needed him in Kiev, then that is where he would preach for God. If God wanted him on a train bringing hope and the light of salvation to those who were discouraged, then that was his assignment. And if God wanted him to be in a prison camp in Siberia, then Siberia it was.

This kind of attitude bolstered Nickolai's faith and gave him courage to face whatever his imagination told him might be coming.

Somewhere in the wee morning hours of the third day, the engineer applied the breaks. As Nickolai stirred, the train slowed and came to a complete stop. The sun hadn't come up yet, but in the dusk of the northern twilight sky, Nickolai could see the landscape clearly.

There was no train station, no village, and not even a sod hut or horse corral. In the glow of the moonlight, it was obvious there was nothing but the mosses, lichens, and scrubby tundra grasses of Western Siberia. The landscape looked to be as desolate as any he had ever seen.

The air was damp and cool. The month of June had come, and with it the longer days of the North Country. In fact, they were so far north that it never really got very dark at night. This time of year the sun set around eleven in the evening, dipping below the northern horizon, and then it came up again around three-thirty in the morning.

The three prisoners climbed out of the train, and with them the two soldiers guarding them. The soldiers pulled half a dozen packs from the mail car and gave them to the prisoners to carry.

As the train pulled away and disappeared to the north, all manacles and handcuffs were removed from the prisoners. Escaping was pointless. They were thousands of kilometers from home and hundreds of kilometers from the nearest train station or remote village.

Andryi, one of the prisoners, grew angry. "We have to walk!" he protested.

"That's right!" One of the guards waved his rifle in Andryi's face. "This is the end of the line for you! The rest of the way is on foot! And in case you haven't noticed," he snorted, "we guards are the ones who should be complaining, not you! We have to walk too, and we're not even criminals."

Andryi scowled at the two soldiers. "Well, how far is it?" he grumbled.

The other soldier stepped forward impatiently. "If we make good time, we can get to the camp by late tonight. And if I were you," he growled, "I wouldn't be thinking about taking too many rest stops. The tundra wolves out here are pretty big. It's June so they might not be that hungry, but we don't want to take any chances. I've seen big ones take down a horse single-handedly."

"Now get going!" the first guard pointed his gun eastward. "The prison camp is that way! March!"

And with that the men walked off into the damp darkness. No flashlights—no torches—only the moon in the southern sky, the dim horizon to the north, and the stars still twinkling in the early morning sky.

CHAPTER 5

The sun rose and the men continued trudging across the Siberian landscape. The weather was pleasant enough, even with the sun shining down in its full strength. A slight breeze was blowing, but not enough to keep the mosquitoes, black flies, and no-see-ums from swarming around the men.

Nickolai and the other men had not taken baths for some time, and this ended up being a natural bug repellent against the insects. The flies and mosquitoes found the smell of sour sweat to be unpleasant and would alight for only a few seconds before moving on.

Unfortunately, this wasn't enough of a deterrent for the no-see-ums—they were the worst. They were so tiny that it was hard to see them, but they were there. They crawled into the men's eyes and ears and noses. They got into the men's hair and under the folds of their clothes. It seemed that no place was off limits to the pesky little insects!

Eventually Nickolai smeared swamp mud on his face, neck, and hands to keep the bugs from biting. When the other men saw the way the mud protected Nickolai, they followed his example.

There was a faint trail across the tundra, which Nickolai felt must be the route to and from the prison camp. It wasn't an easy trail to walk, especially with all the bogs and muskegs everywhere. And skirting the spongy, swampy ground was tiring.

Not a soul appeared to be anywhere in the vicinity. As the day wore on without sign of human life, the strangest sort of panic began to creep over Nickolai. He felt as though he were walking to the edge of the earth's last wilderness where absolute solitude existed. Surely human life could not exist in such a god-forsaken place.

But then he remembered his resolve and his mission. Wherever he was headed, God needed him there. "This gospel of the kingdom shall be preached in all the world, for a witness unto all nations, and then shall the end come." Those were words from one of Nickolai's favorite passages in Scripture, and they reminded him of his commitment to God. The idea calmed him a bit, and after a while, he was able to regain his composure.

The men walked on and on long into the evening, but since the sun set so late this time of year, the way was clearly lit. And then, just as the sun dipped below the horizon, Nickolai caught sight of some buildings in the distance.

The men all quickened their pace. They had come so far. After eleven days of bread and water and handcuffs, their journey was finally over.

As they drew nearer the prison camp and the arctic summer twilight settled in with its deepening shadows, it was still light enough for Nickolai to take stock of the place.

It appeared that the camp had a kitchen and mess hall, and of course barracks for the prisoners to live in. There were other barns and sheds too, and a huge garden, maybe a hectare in size. And sitting prominently in the middle of the camp was a building that looked like some kind of administrative headquarters.

But the thing that surprised Nickolai the most was the building materials. Most of the buildings were not made of wood—they were made of tundra sod. He had heard of such places where the soil, with its grassy roots, was cut out of the ground in blocks and stacked like bricks to make walls, but Nickolai had never actually seen it with his own eyes.

Most of the buildings were made of the sod, except the kitchen and administrative headquarters. What lumber was used in the camp must have been brought in by horse and wagon. There was no other way to get it here, Nickolai figured.

The building construction was quite simple with tall stovepipes sticking through steep corrugated metal roofs designed to shed the heavy Siberian snows. Small doors and very few windows kept the openings in the buildings to a minimum. There was no doubt that this helped conserve the heat Nickolai knew they would need in the long, cold winters ahead.

In front of the building that looked like an administrative headquarters, a USSR flag, with sickle and hammer stitched on it, flapped gently in the breeze. Nickolai sensed that even in this far-flung region, prisoners and guards alike had a sense of patriotism and national pride.

As the party of five arrived in camp, they caused quite a stir. The hour was late, but even so, prisoners and guards alike began to pour out of the barracks and other buildings. It was obvious that most of them had been roused from their sleep, but it didn't seem to matter.

This was the first contact anyone had had with the outside world in months. Everyone gathered around, curious to get a good look at the new prisoners. The soldiers had brought mail for the officers and guards on duty, and there were even a few select pieces for some of the prisoners. But mostly the inmates were just glad to see new faces and hear the latest news.

When all the excitement had died down, the prison warden emerged in a nightshirt. He looked the prisoners over with bloodshot eyes. It looked as if he had been drinking, but Nickolai wasn't surprised. Even in this place there had to be vodka.

There was vodka everywhere in Russia. The people used it to drink away their cares and troubles. They also used it for medicinal purposes, pouring it on cuts and wounds and infections. They even used it in their cars in the winter to keep the radiators and gasoline lines from freezing up.

And surely this prison warden used it to drink away the loneliness of the place. As Nickolai studied the face of the officer, he wondered where this man's family was. Did he have a wife? Did he have children? He looked to be in his early forties. Was he considered a military officer?

The man looked as though he had let his appearance slide, but then again Nickolai had no idea what the standard was for officers in outposts like this one. Did anyone here really care how an officer looked? Nickolai guessed maybe not.

In the glow of twilight, Nickolai could see that the warden's face of stubble already had a head start on the coming day. He had salt-and-pepper hair, and Nickolai had to smile. At least the man still had a full head of hair. Nickolai ran his hand over his own thinning scalp, reminding himself that he had less hair than the warden, though the warden looked to be older.

The warden greeted the prisoners gruffly, and then turned to go back into his own quarters. With a wave of his hand he sent them with a guard on a short tour of the camp.

Nickolai was surprised to discover that there were approximately 300 prisoners at the camp. The prison didn't appear to be big enough for those numbers, but judging by how cramped the bunks were in the barracks, he could believe it. Some 20 to 30 prisoners were crowded into a tiny room large enough for maybe 10 or 12. The only space Nickolai could call his own was his own bunk, which was little more than five feet in length. Rough-hewn boards formed the slats that made up each bunk frame and bed.

Nickolai frowned as he looked around and stared up at the tin roof of the barracks. Like it or not, this was going to be his new home. The sooner he got used to it the better off he'd be.

CHAPTER 6

Near midnight Nickolai finally lay on his bunk, his feet hanging over the end of his bed. Unable to sleep, his mind raced at the strangeness of his new surroundings.

Again, Nickolai was overcome with the remoteness of the place and the very simplicity of the camp. There were no prison walls, no barbed wire, and no guard towers. The guards didn't even carry guns. The very nature of such a prison defied all logic of what could and should be expected in the place.

There was obviously a chain of command from the top on down, as Nickolai was soon to learn. The warden oversaw the prison camp and reported to government officials higher up. Below him were the immediate officers in charge of the various functions of the camp. There were four junior officers. One was in charge of the guards and therefore, indirectly, the prisoners. A second was in charge of work detail units, and so it went.

And prisoners also answered to a pecking order of sorts among their own ranks. Those who had been at the prison camp the longest appeared to have seniority, but not always. If a man was big enough, strong enough, or intimidating enough, he could gain power and prestige among the prisoners.

But no matter the status of a prisoner, escape was out of the question. Nickolai was sure of that. Even in warm weather, to attempt such a thing seemed utterly foolish. Food, for starters would be a problem, even if one could evade the guards who would no doubt be sent out as a posse. How much food would one have to carry in order to survive the march to civilization hundreds and hundreds of kilometers away?

Nickolai knew that wild creatures lived on the open plains, but he had seen very few of them. Reindeer herds ranged the open country, as he had observed while on the moving train, but Nickolai doubted that a lone man on foot with no weapons would be able to catch a reindeer, no matter how desperately he tried.

Of course, there were the tundra wolves, arctic hares, snowy owls, and the many types of lemmings and mice he had been told lived in these parts. But all of them were considered unclean according to biblical standards. Nickolai knew that even if he could catch them, he would never be able to bring himself to eat that kind of meat, no matter how hungry he might be.

The idea of escape was ludicrous at best—and what was the point, anyway? They were all in this remote location together—warden, camp officers, guards, and prisoners. In order to survive the harshness of such an environment, each must do his part, even if there was a pecking order. They needed each another.

And that would have to be enough for now. It was all he could hope for. Here he was in this remote spot in the world, and there was no one he knew. No one to care what happened to him. There was no one it seemed to whom he could speak of loneliness. His fellow prisoners would have to be his confidants and cronies. They would have to be his friends.

But even so, as he tossed and turned, trying to fall asleep, his mind began to panic and scream out in protest, *How did I get myself into this?*

"Please, Lord!" he heard himself begging in whispered tones, "I pray that my time here will not be in vain. May You use me to speak to the other prisoners. May they see Jesus in me. If I can bring the gospel to them and let them see Jesus in me, that would be worth the pain and disappointment of having to be here.

"Let me be a witness to the guards, Lord. Though they mistreat me, let me bear their insults and abuse as You did—without complaining! Let them see that I am different, that the peace of heaven is on my face.

"And the warden? He's a Russian officer schooled in the ways of the military. In his world there is no God. Please, Lord, make him know beyond a shadow of a doubt that You exist. If I can be that person to help him see You and Your saving grace, I would be honored and willing to do that."

Nickolai began to feel the sweet peace of heaven settle over him. It was like a magic potion that had infused his entire body. His prayer in the prison cell and on the train had been that God would be able to use him wherever he happened to be—wherever God could use his service.

"Lord, help me keep up my courage, and let me be faithful to You and the church I love," he breathed. "Here I stand," he quoted the famous words from a book he loved, "I can do no other. May God help me. Amen"

Somewhere in the twilight of the midnight sun, Nickolai finally slept. And then it was morning.

CHAPTER 7

Nickolai sat bolt upright on the wooden boards of the bed where he lay sleeping. He tried to clear the fog from his tired mind to make sense of his surroundings. Where was he? What was he doing here?

"On your feet, men! We don't have all day to lie around spinning dreams! There's work to be done! On your feet!"

Nickolai heard a crash and then a groan just a few feet away. He turned on his bed to see a pile of boards from one of the bunks, and a man underneath them. Above him towered a guard, with shafts of dusty morning sunlight streaming through the open doorway behind him.

Now Nickolai remembered where he was.

The guard strode to where Nickolai was lying, but Nickolai scrambled to his feet and to attention before the guard could take a swipe at him too.

"That's better!" growled the guard in what Nickolai imagined must be a tone of satisfaction. "You've got thirty seconds to line up in front of the cabin! Better yet, let's see you make it in twenty."

Without a second thought Nickolai dashed out into the early morning sun now already well above the northeastern horizon. Even so, the hour was still early. Nickolai figured it couldn't be more than five or five-thirty in the morning.

He squinted at the brightness of the sun and wondered how the sun could rise so early this far north. But of course, with the tilt of the earth's axis during the summer months, places this far north had more daylight than cities farther south like Moscow, or Kiev back home.

When the guard came out of the barracks, Nickolai was still trying to button his shirt and straighten his trousers. It was good that he had boots to wear and not shoes to lace up, or he wouldn't have made it out into the courtyard this fast with all his clothes on.

Nickolai glanced down at his appearance. It was true that his clothes weren't on completely straight, and his shirt wasn't buttoned up all the way, but he was relieved to know that he had somehow managed to straighten himself up in the few seconds the guard had allowed them.

Again Nickolai tried to shake the fog from his eyes and mind. There was no way to escape the reality of his surroundings. He was in a prison camp somewhere in Siberia at the end of a long train ride from the west.

And one thing was sure. If he was going to survive this place of desolation at the ends of the earth, he was going to have to learn to get up on time. Actually, getting up well before he was called would be better.

This was his first morning in camp, and it seemed that he was expected to know everything about the rules and regulations of the place. But Nickolai was quickly learning that one rule seemed to overshadow all others. "Never be late!"

He struggled to think positive thoughts as he stood at attention in the row of prisoners lined up in front of the barracks. The idea of having to do this every morning for the next five years, ten years, or however long it took the KGB authorities to figure they had punished him enough, was almost more than he could bear.

"For being late you boys can skip breakfast this morning!" the guard barked. "That'll teach you to sleep in!"

No one moved.

"Well! What are you waiting for!" he growled as the prisoners stared back at him. "You have your work details! Get to your assignments!"

"You three!" he suddenly added, pointing at Nickolai and the other two new prisoners. "The warden wants to see you immediately!"

The three of them looked at one another with raised eyebrows, but when the guard turned and walked away, they shrugged and simply headed for the administrative building. Nickolai thought it strange that the men in his barracks had been caught sleeping in. Weren't they used to camp life? And weren't they used to getting up this early every morning, or was this just a show of force for Nickolai and the other new prisoners?

And why weren't he and the others being escorted to the warden's quarters? The whole thing seemed kind of strange, but then Nickolai remembered how informal the place was. People were just expected to go about their business and do their jobs, he guessed.

Nickolai was the last of the three to be called into the warden's office. As he stood at attention outside in the hallway, he wondered what went on in these kinds of prisons. What should he expect? Would he be interrogated again? Would he be mistreated because he was a Christian?

When Nickolai finally stood in the warden's office, he was surprised at how simple the place appeared. Though the warden was a colonel in the Russian army, there was almost nothing in his office to dress it up— a medium-sized oak desk, three chairs, a lone kerosene lamp, and a few books on a dusty bookshelf.

After studying an official letter that had been sent him via the mailbag on the train, the warden cleared his throat. "You had a run-in with the KGB."

Nickolai waited but said nothing since the warden's statement was more commentary than anything.

"Nickolai Panchuk," the warden put the official letter back in a folder on his desk, "I've got no use for preachers! As far as I'm concerned, you preachers are all just a bunch of rebels!"

The warden brought his fist down on the desk with a bang. "You think you can change the world!" he growled. "Well, I've got news for you! The motherland is fine the way she is! The Union of Soviet Socialists Republic is the greatest nation the world has ever known! She doesn't need any help!" The warden squinted at Nickolai through slit eyes. "Do you understand that, Panchuk?"

"Yes, sir!" Even though Nickolai was a Christian and didn't agree with the tactics the government used, he was still proud to be a citizen of the USSR. It made his chest swell just to hear the national anthem or see athletes competing for the glory of the motherland.

The officer leaned back in his chair. "I'll tell you what, Panchuk." He seemed to cool a bit. "Let's forget about what it was that got you here in the first place. If you follow my orders in this camp, I'll not give you any trouble. We'll let bygones be bygones. What do you say to that?"

The warden began sorting through some other papers on his desk.

Nickolai wondered whether the warden fully understood the charges being brought against him? He had to, didn't he? The man had Nickolai's file! Did he know about the secret churches? Would he be expecting Nickolai to give him the list of church members?

Of course, Nickolai knew he would never give such a list to the warden! Not even if the warden should beat him! Not even if the warden should kill him. But of course the warden didn't know that. Nickolai wondered if he should just bring up the subject and get it all out in the open now. On the other hand, maybe he should just let the warden figure it out for himself.

"I want to cooperate, sir!" Nickolai's face was stolid as he stood at attention and stared straight ahead.

The warden stood to his feet suddenly. "Good, Nickolai. I'm glad to hear that." A slight grin edged the corners of his mouth. "Now, I'm sending you to the wood shop. You'll be working with Vadeem, the camp carpenter. Lots of work to do around here," he announced.

"And remember, Panchuk," he added as he pointed the way for Nickolai, "follow orders, and you and I will get along just fine."

CHAPTER 8

Nickolai couldn't believe his ears. That was it? No interrogation? No grilling to get long-sought-after information from "the preacher"?

This was too good to be true. It couldn't be that easy, and Nickolai was sure there would be future confrontations.

As he turned to go, Nickolai suddenly remembered his biggest problem of all—the Sabbath. He would be required to work during Sabbath hours. That's what happened when you were a prisoner.

Nickolai wondered. Should he say something about it now or wait until Saturday when the Sabbath would actually become an issue?

Instinctively Nickolai knew he'd better take care of it immediately while he still had the courage and the warden's attention.

"Sir," Nickolai stopped and turned around. "There is one thing that may be a problem."

But already the warden had moved on to other things. "Remember, Panchuk. No problems. Simply obey orders, and you and I will get along fine."

And with that the warden waved him out the door.

Nickolai stood a few moments longer wondering what he should do, but he realized there was no use pressing the issue now. The warden was in no mood to listen, and maybe it wasn't the right time for such a discussion anyway. God had His own timetable as to when these things should be taken care of, Nickolai mused. He knew he'd better let God work everything out as He saw best. Help me know when that time is, he silently prayed.

Nickolai went looking for Vadeem and found him in the wood shop. The camp carpenter still had the pungent odor of garlic on his breath, and the smell of it made Nickolai ravenous. Garlic was one of his favorite foods, and knowing that he had been deprived of breakfast made it twice as hard to go to work and wait for the mid-day meal.

But Vadeem had plenty for Nickolai to do, and that made him almost forget the grumbling, growling feeling in his stomach. The mess hall needed more wooden benches made. Then there were the few boards in the floor of the administrative headquarters that needed to be replaced, and a door at the mess hall needed mending.

Lunch finally came. It was a simple one, but Nickolai didn't care. He was just glad to get something warm into his stomach. The cook had made borsch with beets, onions, and cabbage in it. It was the most heavenly food Nickolai could remember tasting. And the Russian black bread tasted like cake to Nickolai after his days on the train with so little to eat.

That afternoon Vadeem told Nickolai they needed to repair some of the large wooden water barrels sitting near the kitchen. Each barrel held about fifty gallons of water and was made with oak staves. Nickolai had to tip them on their side to roll them back to the woodshop where Vadeem would be making the repairs.

On his trip back for the second barrel, Nickolai noticed that an ox cart had pulled up at the kitchen. The cart held two large wooden barrels filled with water hauled from a spring located more than a kilometer away. Oleg, the driver of the ox cart, was shouting at the ox trying to get him to pull the cart forward a bit more so the water could be hauled inside the kitchen, but the ox wouldn't budge a step further.

Maybe the ox was tired from hauling the water, and maybe he was just being plain stubborn. Or maybe he was weary of the treatment he had been receiving from the driver.

At any rate, it was obviously a showdown, and it seemed both the driver and ox were determined to win. When the driver pulled out his leather prod and began to whip the ox in the face, Nickolai sprang into action. He knew it probably wasn't wise to get involved since this was only his first day in camp, but he couldn't bear to see the animal being mistreated.

"Hold on!" he called to the driver. "It's obvious the ox is too stubborn for his own good! Why don't we try something else?"

Nickolai tried not to look at the driver. He was butting in where he might not be wanted, but he felt he had to try.

"What's his name?" Nickolai asked nonchalantly, as he stepped up to the ox and gave the animal a pat on his thick, muscled neck.

"Maksim, I guess," the prisoner replied. "I never use that name, but I guess it's his name."

"Animals are like people," Nickolai said. "They like to be convinced to do something—not beaten into submission."

Nickolai patted the ox's neck again and leaned forward to whisper something into its ear. Then he took hold of a halter around the ox's neck and pulled forward as he continued talking to the ox.

The technique did the trick. In a matter of seconds, the ox had pulled the cart a few meters forward so the driver could unload the barrels and put them on pallets outside the kitchen.

That night after the evening meal Nickolai went to the stables where he found Maksim quietly munching on tundra marsh grass. Nickolai sat down beside the big animal and watched him eat. He felt sorry for him. In some ways he thought he understood how Maksim must feel. The ox's job was to work every day, day in and day out, week after week, with no break. That seemed to be his only purpose in life.

And he was a prisoner like Nickolai. He was not his own boss. He couldn't come and go as he pleased. His job was to haul water from the spring, and it probably would be until the day he died.

After that first evening visit with Maksim, Nickolai stopped by the stables every night to bring the ox a little something from the kitchen. Sometimes it was a beet or a wedge of cabbage. Sometimes it was just a small carrot, but it was the talks he had with Maksim that helped Nickolai the most.

Nickolai was sure that he was getting much more from the visits than Maksim was, but the animal seemed to enjoy the company. The one-sided conversations helped Nickolai deal with the pain of being so far from home. When he felt he was going to panic from the loneliness that threatened to overwhelm him, old Maksim would look at him with his big brown eyes and just listen.

And so a relationship began to grow between Nickolai and Maksim. It was a wonderful tonic for Nickolai's spirit, and it helped him deal with the discouragement of those first few days in camp.

SDO-2

CHAPTER 9

As the week progressed, Nickolai knew the Sabbath problem wasn't going to go away. He was going to have to face it. Several times he wondered how he should break the news to the warden, but there seemed to be no good way to do it, and no good time either. The warden kept to himself and didn't invite many visitors to his office. One thing was sure. He had Nickolai's file in his office, and sooner or later it would probably be used against him.

The Sabbath hadn't been a specific problem on Nickolai's record—the thing that had gotten him into trouble had been his unwillingness to cooperate with the KGB and give them a list of his church members. But would the Sabbath be a problem now? Nickolai could hardly imagine that it wouldn't, since the warden had reminded him that obeying the camp rules was extremely important. And Nickolai hadn't heard that there were any days off for rest or recreation.

As Thursday and then Friday came, Nickolai knew a showdown was imminent.

On Sabbath morning, long before the roosters were crowing over in the chicken coop, Nickolai was up, restless and waiting for the will of God to be revealed. "What is it You have in store for me?" Nickolai whispered as he knelt in the early morning shadows of the sod barracks. "I know You want me to be Your witness, and I know I may have to suffer for Your sake, but how am I to know Your plans for me?"

But the voice of God was strangely silent, and Nickolai knew that this one of those times when he would simply have to wait for God to lead.

When he heard the other prisoners in his barracks begin to stir, he knew the time was fast approaching. And since God had not told him what to do, Nickolai made a decision—he would go out to role call, but not to breakfast or his work assignment. After role call he would return to the barracks to fast and pray. Come what may, this was his decision, and he would stick by it.

And that was it. It was as though God had been waiting for Nickolai to make a decision about the Sabbath and then act on it. It was this moment of decision that gave Nickolai the confidence he had been lacking all week. Suddenly he could see things clearly as though a window of opportunity had opened.

He was standing on the threshold of another great moment in his life. He sensed that things were going to be very hard for him now that he had made this decision, but he wanted to go through with it anyway.

After role call he did exactly as he had planned. He returned to the barracks, knelt down again on the hard dirt floor by his bunk, and began to pray. And every moment that passed took him closer to the inevitable confrontation he knew was coming.

But it didn't come as soon as he had expected, and he should have guessed as much. No one would know that he hadn't shown up for his work assignment except Vadeem, and the carpenter might simply think that Nickolai had been asked to work somewhere else for the day.

But finally, the moment of truth arrived. About mid-morning Nickolai heard one of the guards outside talking to another prisoner.

"Where's Panchuk!" the gravelly voice demanded.

"I haven't seen him," came the reply.

It was almost noon before Nickolai was finally discovered in the barracks, and when he was it seemed the whole world was caving in.

"What are you doing here?" the guard demanded. "Are you sick?"

Nickolai knew that if he said he was sick, they might let him off for the day, but that wouldn't fix the problem. The following week, he would be in the barracks again, and the likelihood of his being sick two Sabbaths in a row would certainly be cause for suspicion. Nickolai knew he needed to deal with the Sabbath issue now. He needed to face this problem head on no matter what the consequences. It was the only way.

"I'm not sick," Nickolai said plainly, getting to his feet.

"Then why are you in here!" the guard asked incredulously as though expecting some sort of ridiculous answer. And he got one.

"I can't work today because it's the seventh-day Sabbath of the Lord my God."

"The seventh-day what!" the guard yelled, standing stock-still.

"The seventh day is God's holy Sabbath, and I'm forbidden to work on it. The Bible is very—"

"The Bible!" Nickolai was cut short by the guard. It was obvious the guard hadn't seen this coming, and it gave Nickolai a chance to take the explanation a bit further.

"The Bible is God's Holy Word, and in it He tells me I should worship Him on the seventh-day Sabbath in honor of the world's creation." Nickolai would have liked to say more, but he knew the guard would never let him finish, and he was right.

"I don't know what you're talking about!" the guard interrupted again, finally getting his bearings. "It doesn't matter what day it is! We work every day around here! On your feet Panchuk! I won't have any slackers in these barracks!"

But Nickolai made no move to go, and this infuriated the guard even more.

"I'll teach you to disobey orders!" he shouted again, his face turning purple with rage. He pulled a nightstick from his belt and began to beat Nickolai on the head and shoulders.

Nickolai didn't have time to do anything but cover his head with his hands and arms. It hurt, but he was able to deflect the worst blows of the beating.

"Now get to your work assignment!" the guard shouted. "Vadeem is looking for you!" Both Nickolai and the guard were breathing hard by now, but Nickolai still made no move to go.

"I'm sorry, but I can't work," Nickolai repeated the words quietly. "It's forbidden for me to work on God's holy day."

At this the guard let loose with a steady stream of curses and began to beat Nickolai mercilessly with his fists. Then he grabbed Nickolai by his shirt collar and dragged him out the door into the barracks courtyard.

By now the commotion was so great that other prisoners were looking toward them to see what the noise was all about.

"We'll see about this seven day holy Sabbath of yours!" he shouted uncontrollably. "We'll just take you to the warden and see what he says about all this! He'll know what to do with the likes of you!"

CHAPTER 10

Moments later Nickolai was in front of the warden's office. Although he was still standing, he was a sorry sight. His face was beginning to swell from the beating he had received to his head. One eye was turning black, his shirt was almost ripped off, and his hair was all covered with dirt and straw.

"What's the meaning of this!" the warden demanded, coming out of his office. When he saw Nickolai, he began to walk round and round him.

"He insists that he can't work today because it's some kind of a holy day!" snapped the guard.

"A holy day, is it? Well now, Yuri," the warden turned to the guard. "I see that you tried to enlighten this man on the ways of our camp. You are to be commended."

By now Nickolai could hardly see through the eye that was swelling shut. He was indeed suffering for the decision he had made to keep God's Sabbath holy, but it didn't matter. This was a small price to pay compared to the suffering that Jesus had endured for Nickolai. What harm could it do to suffer a little for Him?

The warden turned back to Nickolai. "What have you got to say for yourself, troublemaker?"

"It's true," Nickolai admitted. Although he could not see clearly, he stared straight ahead again, not looking directly at the warden.

"Well, I hope you've learned your lesson," his voice sounded as smooth as syrup, as he came to stand in front of Nickolai, but beneath it all Nickolai sensed the man could be cruel.

"Are you ready to go back to work?" He stood toe to toe with the prisoner, his nose barely inches from Nickolai's face.

"It's God's holy day. I cannot work on the seventh-day Sabbath."

The warden's eyes grew steely cold. "You can't work?" he asked plainly, his voice strangely calm, but Nickolai could tell there was disdain beneath the calm exterior, and he sensed that the worst was yet to come.

"Not on God's holy day."

"Is that your final answer?"

"Yes, sir."

"The consequences will be severe." The warden's voice was still even, but the tension was building.

"It's my decision, sir. I'm willing to take the punishment."

"And you will." The warden turned to Yuri with ice in his voice, and he had a cold gleam in his eye. "Go get my whip from my office. Strip the preacher to the waist and tie him to the flagpole. We'll see how strong this boy is."

Nickolai was brave, but he found it difficult to keep from crying out in pain. The warden did indeed make a spectacle of Nickolai as he beat him mercilessly with the whip. Finally Nickolai slumped to the ground unconscious, and it was only then that the warden stopped long enough to catch his breath.

He wiped the sweat from his forehead and handed the whip to Yuri. "Cut him loose. When he comes to, he can find his own way back to the barracks."

And with that the warden went back inside his office. Yuri watched him go, not surprised, but a bit solemn at this display of the warden's fury. It had been a long time since he had seen the warden beat a prisoner like this, and it was a bit disturbing for him to see the warden enjoy it so.

He himself had beaten Nickolai just minutes before, but now he realized what anger could do to someone if unchecked. It was a rather strange mixture of feelings, and he was hard pressed to explain the anger that he and the warden felt toward these prisoners.

How long Nickolai lay on the ground he didn't know. The sun was low in the sky when he finally came to, and he could hardly move. The blood had dried on his back, but the flies were having a feast. After a bit he finally managed to stand and slowly stagger back to the barracks. When he got there, he collapsed on his bunk and fell into an exhausted sleep.

The next day his back felt like chopped meat, but he managed to get to his feet. He was able to wash the blood from his face, but he couldn't reach his back. His shirt covered the lacerations on his back, but his face was black and blue for all to see.

And not surprisingly, the other prisoners avoided him. It was too risky to do otherwise. After all, who would want to befriend a foolish preacher who would rather be horse whipped than give in to the warden's demands? Any one of them might be considered a sympathizer if they were caught talking to Nickolai.

During the next few days, Nickolai grew stronger. The wounds healed slowly, but his courage grew with each day. He had passed the test. He had been strong for Jesus. He had not given in even though he knew he would suffer for it.

As the days passed, the other prisoners still avoided him, but he thought he saw faint looks of admiration directed toward him. Tuesday came and went, and then Wednesday and Thursday. Nickolai began to think of the coming Sabbath. What would be his fate? Would the warden respect him for his stand on the Sabbath? Would he grant him the privilege to rest as he had asked?

Or would it be just the opposite? Would he get another beating for his decision to honor the Sabbath?

Unfortunately, Nickolai couldn't see that worse was still to come, and it was just as well. He needed to grow a bit stronger before Satan's tide of evil would again hit him with all its force.

CHAPTER 11

All week Nickolai worried about what would happen on Sabbath morning. He knew he shouldn't worry, but he dreaded what might be coming next. He thought he would be willing to take more of the same treatment he had already received, but his wounds hadn't healed yet from the warden's initial horse whipping. If he was whipped again, the wounds would just open up again, and he could only imagine what the pain would be like then.

By Friday night, though, his faith was strong, and he was determined to stand for God and face whatever was in store for him tomorrow. If God would give him the courage and the strength to go on, Nickolai was determined to be faithful to God no matter what happened.

Sabbath dawned cool and clear. Nickolai didn't know how early he had awakened. He didn't have a watch, but he could tell by the snoring in the barracks that it was early—well before the usual time to rise.

Because of the lacerations and bruises on his back, Nickolai had been sleeping on his stomach, but now he rolled out of bed and onto his knees.

"Please Lord!" he prayed. "Let me be worthy of the persecution that might come my way today. I know it's a small thing compared to what You did for me, but I'll gladly do it."

How long he stayed on his knees, he couldn't say, but suddenly Yuri's gravelly voice was waking everyone in the barracks as though it were the judgment day.

"On your feet, men! Out of those beds!"

Yuri gave a few of the beds a jarring kick, sending prisoners flying out of them in a hurry.

Nickolai jumped to his feet too, but not before Yuri noticed him.

"Well, now, Panchuk! It's nice to see that we're not going to have any foolishness this morning. I can see that you've come to your senses!"

Nickolai smiled weakly, but said nothing. He knew trouble was already on its way, but what should he say? No matter what he said, the whole thing was going to blow up in his face.

All the soldiers filed out into the morning sunshine and waited for their orders after role call. The officer in charge of camp maintenance and repairs read down through a list of the tasks for the day. Several of the prisoners in Nickolai's barracks were to work with a crew that would be helping to butcher some reindeer meat brought in the day before. The dozen or so animals had somehow split off from a larger herd and migrated west toward the camp where the guards spotted them though field glasses.

Other prisoners were sent to cut new sod to build yet another barracks that was soon to go up. It had been rumored that another batch of prisoners would be coming in the next month, and the current barracks were already bursting to overflowing.

"And Panchuk?" Yuri looked straight at Nickolai. "You are to report to Vadeem immediately after breakfast. He needs to do some roof repairs on the mess hall."

Nickolai looked straight ahead. The moment he feared most had arrived, and of course he wasn't surprised. Would the confrontations and beatings start all over again?

"Well! What are you waiting for?" Yuri demanded as Nickolai looked straight ahead and didn't offer to move.

He opened his mouth to speak, but then closed it again. What was the use? They were going to mistreat him anyway, no matter what he said.

But then he remembered his promise to God that he would speak for the Lord wherever he was sent, or in whatever he was asked to do.

Nickolai took a deep breath. "I can't work today because it's the seventh-day Sabbath of the Lord my God."

The guard's face took on a shocked look of exasperation, but then turned to annoyance.

"Preacher man! You have got to be kidding!" he blurted. The other prisoners stared at Nickolai and shook their heads silently.

Yuri finally overcame his silence and snorted, "So you've decided to be stupid again, have you? Well, we'll see about that!"

He grabbed Nickolai by the arm and marched him off to the warden's office, and then left him standing in the hallway just outside the imposing doorway.

Nickolai finally dredged up enough courage to knock on the door. Maybe the warden wasn't in, Nickolai hoped. Maybe he was busy doing something more important.

But soon the door opened, and when the warden saw Nickolai, a look of disbelief came across his face.

"What do you want, Panchuk?" he shook his head pathetically. "Don't tell me! You've decided to be stubborn again!" The warden came right to the point. It was as if he had somehow known all along that Nickolai would refuse to work again come Saturday but had never really allowed himself to imagine it.

Nickolai opened his mouth to speak again, but the warden cut him off.

"Alright! If that's the way you want it! Come with me!" he stood to his feet, stepped through the open doorway, and then down the short hallway.

Nickolai stood rooted to the spot as he watched the warden go.

CHAPTER 12

The warden turned impatiently. "Panchuk! Get a move on it!" he snapped. "Try to keep up!"

Nickolai hurriedly fell in step behind the warden as they exited the building. What would happen next? Was he going to be given a pass from work for the day? Was he going to be allowed to rest and worship according to his convictions?

The warden walked to one of the sod sheds and opened the door. It was the stables where old Maksim was kept, and it smelled of it. There were no windows in the building so the inside appeared dark and foreboding. This didn't look good. Undoubtedly, for Nickolai things were going from bad to worse. Was he going to be beaten again? Was he going to be tortured? Nickolai cringed. Was he going to be executed?

Suddenly Nickolai began to panic. During his early morning prayers, his imagination had run wild with all kinds of abuse that he knew they could heap on him, but he hadn't really thought of death. Not really. Death had always seemed so remote out here where there was so much work to be done. In a camp like this where the prisoners did all the work, executing a prisoner seemed so pointless.

Nickolai knew this kind of logic bordered on insanity. He had to get a grip. He watched as the warden walked to a corner of the dark stables where a large wooden box sat. It didn't look to be more than a meter long or high, and possibly half a meter wide.

Nickolai's heart began to hammer wildly in his chest like a caged animal. Was this the end? He tried to calm his racing heart, but there was no time to think. No time to collect his wits.

Then he remembered his prayer that morning and his promise to God. He had pledged himself to suffer anything for God, so why not now? Why not this? Whatever the warden had in store for him, it couldn't be worse than what Jesus had suffered for him.

The warden lifted the top off the wooden box. Even in the dim shadows of the sod stable, Nickolai could see that the box was empty.

"Get in," the warden ordered.

"Get in?" Nickolai echoed.

The warden didn't reply, but motioned with his head toward the crate.

"The box? I'm supposed to get in the box?"

"Do I need to spell it out for you! Yes, you're supposed to get in the box!" The stables echoed the stillness of the moment. "Now get moving! I don't have all day!"

Nickolai took one last look at the warden and then stepped toward the box. He lifted a leg and got inside—it was smaller than it looked.

"Sit down!" the warden ordered.

As the lid slammed down over him, a shower of dust choked Nickolai, making him wheeze.

"Hope you like your new home," the warden called as he turned to go.

The wooden slats of the box were thick so it looked like it would be next to impossible to break his way out. And besides, what would it accomplish. The warden would just build a stronger box to hold him.

He had heard of boxes like this one being used to keep prisoners locked up, but this box had so many cobwebs it didn't look like it had been used in years. Maybe the box was used for the hardest of criminals. Maybe the other prisoners just behaved themselves and didn't get themselves into predicaments like Nickolai had.

The light from the open doorway told Nickolai that there were cracks in the sides of the box. He would have no problem breathing, but keeping his legs from cramping up was going to be a trick. He couldn't stand up and he couldn't lie down, so he couldn't stretch his legs out.

Nickolai wanted to give up in despair, but he knew that wasn't an option. Not when he had promised himself that he was going to be true to God and be His steadfast witness. Suffering was the least of his worries. Failing to trust in God was a bigger concern right now.

Nickolai closed his eyes and leaned against the inside wall of the box. He knew this was not going to be a pleasant experience. In fact, it promised to be downright excruciating. How long would they wait before they let him out of the box? Days? Weeks? Would they bring him food? Would they give him water? Would they let him out to go to the bathroom?

"Please Lord, don't let me become discouraged," he prayed. "Don't let my faith in You fail."

As the hours slowly passed, the light in the stable doorway changed direction and then finally began to grow dim. About that time Oleg, the ox cart driver, came into the shed leading old Maksim. Oleg gave the animal food and water, and then left. Nickolai thought Oleg might at least have offered him some water, but then realized that he should have asked. What had he been thinking? Oleg probably didn't even know that Nickolai was locked in the box in the shed.

"Hello, Maksim," Nickolai finally called to the ox, trying to cheer himself up. "I hope your day was better than mine."

As Nickolai sat in the box, he could hear the old ox munching the sedge grass in his manger. He thought about how hard the ox had to work as a beast of burden every day, and he even found himself feeling sorry for the ox.

Right now, though, he thought he would gladly change places with the ox. Even if he had to pull an ox cart loaded with water barrels all the way from the spring a kilometer away, it would be better than sitting in this box all day.

CHAPTER 13

As darkness settled in, the mosquitoes came in droves. They bit at Nickolai's neck and face until he finally stopped swatting at them and gave up the fight. Right now the worst thing about being in the box was the mosquitoes, but he sensed that not being able to stretch his legs was going to be a nightmare.

Eventually he dozed. He didn't sleep well with the mosquitoes everywhere, but he did doze off.

Somewhere in the night he awoke and couldn't go back to sleep. His mouth was dry—he hadn't had water all day, and he wondered when they would bring him some. Had the guards forgotten that he would need water? He was hungry too—who could say when he'd get a chance to eat again?

But it was the circulation in his legs that worried him most. By now his ankles and feet felt numb with stiffness from his legs being bent up so close to his body. He tried to get the blood flowing in his legs, but it was difficult because the box was so small. There just wasn't room enough to stretch out inside the box.

At times like this he wished that he were a smaller man. If he hadn't felt so miserable, Nickolai might have smiled at such a thought. Being a bit shorter would have allowed him some room to get more exercise in the small box.

But there was to be no relief for the numbness that kept coming back to his lower legs. Finally, he began to pray again as he had done a dozen times since being locked up in the box. It was the only thing that made him feel better. That and the verses of Scripture he quoted to bring himself comfort.

When the sun finally came up, he felt like it had been the longest night of his life. When Oleg came to get Maksim, Nickolai asked him if he could have some water. Oleg was startled to hear Nickolai's voice from the box.

"What are you doing in there?" Oleg asked, peering into the shadows. "Did the warden put you in that box?"

"He did." Nickolai felt a bit embarrassed, but he decided he wouldn't try to hide the reason why. "I refused to work yesterday on the Sabbath, so he put me in here to punish me."

"I heard that you had been punished, but I didn't know where you were." Oleg shook his head. "I'd better not give you water. They might not like it."

"Can you ask one of the guards to bring me some, then. I think they may have forgotten me here. No one's been out here except you since they put me in here yesterday."

"I'll see what I can do."

But the guards never came with any water, or any food for that matter, either. All day Nickolai worked to keep his legs moving, and all day he prayed. By now he knew that his time in the box was going to be a long ordeal. He didn't quite know what to expect because the warden didn't say how long he would have to stay in the box.

Every time he heard footsteps he thought it might be someone coming to bring him water or food, or to let him out of the box to stretch.

Sometime late that afternoon a guard did come into the shed to give Nickolai a can of water, but no food. The water felt cool and wet to his parched lips and throat—and yet thirsty as he was, Nickolai wisely decided to save some of the water for later.

Oleg came in with Maksim later that night, and again Nickolai was glad to have the company of someone to talk to, even if it was just an ox.

The night passed in extreme discomfort. The mosquitoes made it almost impossible for him to sleep, and of course the numbing pain in his legs was the worst of all.

Nickolai wished that he could get out of the box to use a bathroom, but no one let him out, so the box soon developed an unpleasant odor. Unfortunately there was nothing Nickolai could do about it.

The hours slowly passed with Oleg and Maksim leaving early the next morning, and then returning again sometime before dark. A guard came with water again, but still no food. Night came once more, and by now it took all Nickolai's faith and energy just to pray. Did anyone care about him? Was there no value to his life?

And what about God? Did He care that Nickolai was suffering? Nickolai knew the answer to that last question, but he was really feeling sorry for himself by now. God could help relieve his suffering, but He was not choosing to do so right now. There had to be a good reason, of course.

Through all these long days filled with pain and loneliness and frustrated faith, Nickolai held to the Scripture promises he had always believed in. Satan wanted to make him suffer, but God loved him more than he could possibly imagine. There was a battle going on between good and evil, a war zone in which Nickolai was suffering as much pain and persecution as Satan could muster.

Jesus suffered for me with pain that was indescribable. Why should my experience for Him be any different? Nickolai tried to bolster his courage with these thoughts, but it was difficult.

As with the story of Job, Nickolai knew that some pain and heartache could not be explained except in light of the invisible war going on in the supernatural world. When he thought about it in this way, it seemed to help more than anything else.

One thing was for sure. While Nickolai was locked up in the box, he could have his Sabbath rest. It wasn't exactly the place he would have chosen to spend the Lord's day, but at least he didn't have to work. No matter how Nickolai looked at it, he had to admit it was a blessing in disguise.

CHAPTER 14

The weekend passed and Monday came and went. By now the thought of food had almost gone from Nickolai's mind. He had not eaten in nine days. It was as if his body had slipped into another world that no longer required him to eat. Of course he was getting weaker every day, but being in the box didn't require much movement, so it also required very little energy.

However, there was a dull throbbing pain in his legs, and that scared Nickolai more than anything. During the first few days in the box, the pain had been pretty bad whenever he moved his legs. Now he couldn't make them move of their own accord. It was as if they were logs of wood attached to his body at the hips—he couldn't really feel them much anymore. He worked on them all the time, using his arms to move them every day, many times a day.

By Tuesday of the second week the box smelled rank beyond description, and the flies were everywhere. It was a living nightmare. Nickolai no longer worried about the warden. He no longer worried about food or water. He just prayed that God would give him the strength to make it through another day.

Around noon on the tenth day, Nickolai heard footsteps. He peered through the slats and saw the warden standing in the doorway. Yuri, the barracks guard, was with him.

"Open the box," the warden said. That was all. It was as if this were a mere formality in the life and duties of a warden at the prison camp.

To Nickolai it had been the worst experience of his life.

Yuri opened the lid of the box. "Oh my!" he sputtered as he held his hand over his mouth. "You smell putrid! Get out of the box!" he ordered, shaking his head in disgust. "You're free to go!"

But Nickolai couldn't stand.

Yuri reached down and lifted Nickolai out of the box. When he saw that Nickolai couldn't walk, his face grew serious, and a look of compassion filled his eyes. He helped Nickolai to a bed of straw and let him lay down.

"I'll be all right," Nickolai assured him with a weak smile. Right now he just wanted to be alone so that he could scream out in pain if he needed to. For ten days he hadn't been able to move his legs properly, and now the pain of moving them was almost as excruciating as having his legs cramped up in the box.

All the rest of that day Nickolai lay on the straw trying to gain his strength and flex his legs so that he could walk on them. Yuri brought him a tin plate of borsch at the supper hour, and Nickolai managed to eat a few bites—he wasn't foolish enough to eat it all. After being deprived of food for so long, he knew his stomach would never be able to handle that much food.

Before dusk, Oleg and Maksim came in from their long day of hauling water. Once again Nickolai felt a sense of kingship with the ox and was glad for his company. As the night settled in, Nickolai didn't even try to go to the barracks, but stayed in the stables with Maksim instead. In fact, when the ox finally lay down in the straw, Nickolai crawled over to warm himself by the animal's big body.

Nickolai then dropped into a sleep so deep that he never even noticed the mosquitoes swarming around him. Surprisingly, they didn't bother him much that night. Maybe it was the fact that he smelled so bad.

The next morning Nickolai felt much better. He could stand some and even walk a bit. The guard brought more food for him—a bowl of borsch and some Russian black bread. Again Nickolai was careful about the amount he ate, but he did manage to eat more than he had the day before.

He cleaned up and then went back to work with Vadeem, though he found he couldn't lift much of anything. He didn't have any strength in his arms or legs, and he tired easily.

"Not surprising!" Vadeem looked at Nickolai as if the preacher man were crazy. "You must have a death wish!" he chided. "Whatever would possess you to put yourself through ten days of torture in that box!"

Nickolai tried to explain about his love for God, and God's love for the human race. He tried to explain about his sacred devotion to the Sabbath. But Vadeem just shook his head in disbelief and muttered to himself under his breath.

By Thursday morning, Nickolai could get around pretty well, though he did have a limp in his stride. Friday arrived and for the first time since he had been pulled from the box, Nickolai allowed himself to think about what the next morning might bring. To him Sabbath was a very special day, whether he was in a church or a lonely prison camp. However, Sabbath also meant that he was going to have to face the warden again. What would the high-ranking officer do this time?

The first time Nickolai had been severely beaten by both Yuri and the warden. The second Sabbath they had locked him up in a box for ten days. On the third time around would they finally give up, or would the persecutions continue?

Nickolai wondered how much worse things could get. He was sure that there would be another confrontation with the warden, and he dreaded it, but he also knew that he had to remain faithful to God no matter what. He couldn't give up now. The Sabbath was his special blessing from God. With all his heart he wanted to honor the sacred day and the Creator God who had designed it.

CHAPTER 15

The night was moving slowly into the first shades of dawn when Nickolai suddenly awoke. What it was that had awakened him he couldn't say. It wasn't the noise of anyone else in the barracks. They were all still sleeping, though Nickolai was sure their laborious snoring could have kept him awake all night if he hadn't been so tired.

It wasn't the sound of birds. There were very few songbirds out here on the Siberian steppes.

Nickolai wondered if it was his mind working overtime that had woken him with a start. And what could he expect. The ordeal through which he had been during the past two weeks had been horrible! Dreadfully uncomfortable!

And what about the next go-around with the warden? Nickolai feared it would be as bad as the times before. Maybe worse.

But he was calm—surprisingly so, and it felt strange. To be sure, he didn't relish the idea of spending more time in a box, if that's what the warden had in store for him, but for some reason Nickolai didn't feel like he needed to escape the approaching hardship the warden might bring. In fact, he felt very little anxiety over it.

So why couldn't he sleep then? Maybe he just needed more strength, the kind of strength he could only get through prayer.

Nickolai slipped out of bed and on to his knees to pray to his heavenly Father. It was wonderful to be able to call on the One who could give him help in time of need—wonderful to feel the presence of the Holy Spirit kneeling with him on the hard dirt floor beside that narrow bunk.

The longer he prayed, the more sure he was that he was going to have to suffer more. He would not be delivered from trouble. He would not be spared humiliation and pain. That's not the way it had usually worked for Nickolai, and he was okay with that right now. His faith might falter when he was tired, or lonely, or weak, but this morning in the cool dawn of the Siberian summer everything was going to be alright.

All too soon the sun rose and the five o'clock wake-up call came from the guards. The prisoners in the barracks slowly stirred and then rolled out of bed to avoid having the guards come in and flush them out.

For Nickolai another Sabbath day had dawned, and again he found himself at attention, standing in front of the bunkhouse. Again Yuri dismissed the men after roll call, but this time he kept his eye on Nickolai.

Nickolai knew it was pointless to prolong the agony of the moment. He didn't make a move, and of course Yuri noticed it. He came to where Nickolai was standing and stood with his big feet planted wide in front of the prisoner.

"Please don't tell me that you're going to refuse to work again!" he demanded in exasperation, "Because if it's true, I think I've probably met the dumbest men alive!"

Yuri continued to stare at Nickolai with something akin to awe on his face. He tried to hide it, but it remained there long enough to make them both uncomfortable.

And then the guard appeared to regain his composure as he seemed to brush the feeling off. "Forget it!" he half shouted. "Just get over to the warden's office right now!"

Nickolai knew Yuri was angry, and really, he had a right to be. What did he know of Nickolai or his God? What did he know of the love of a Creator for His children, and the devotion Nickolai felt for this God who had come to die for man? All Yuri knew was that this stubborn Christian pastor was making trouble and upsetting the routine of the camp.

Within seconds Nickolai had crossed the compound and was waiting in the doorway of the warden's office.

"What are you doing here, Panchuk?" The warden's eyes narrowed with surprise and skepticism and anger all in the same moment.

But Nickolai said nothing. He just stood at attention, his eyes focused forward. What could he say?

"I asked you a question, preacher man!"

Nickolai knew he dared not wait to answer the irate warden. But how could he make the warden understand why he wanted to honor the seventh day of the week. The warden was the product of a society that taught that there was no such thing as a loving personal God. He had been working in the military for decades and was indoctrinated with the concept that the only real answer to life was military force.

"I can't work today, sir," Nickolai began. "I can't dishonor God's holy Sabbath day."

The warden's face contorted with rage. He ground his teeth together and then brought a fist down on his desk.

"You're impossible, Panchuk! I have never in all my days met a man with your stubborn stupidity!" He rose to his feet and pushed Nickolai back out through the open doorway!

"Guard!" he shouted, looking down the hallway. "Get this man out of my office and take him back to the box!" The sound of running footsteps could be heard, and then Yuri was there, a look of disbelief on his face.

"Take Panchuk back to the box, Yuri. He likes it so much he wants to spend another ten days there."

Yuri hung his head, and then finally motioned for Nickolai to follow him to the stable. When they arrived at the box, he lifted the lid and motioned with his head for Nickolai to get in.

When the lid dropped down on Nickolai and the dust had settled, the "preacher man" had time to think about his decision.

He wasn't sorry. He had no regrets. He knew being locked in the box was going to be uncomfortable and excruciating, but he wasn't worried. For some strange reason he felt no anxiety or fear or dread of the next ten days to come. It was all so bizarre; he couldn't explain it.

Some days he knew he was going to feel abandoned and alone, no doubt, but right here and now he was determined that he wouldn't lay the blame on God. It wasn't the Lord's fault that he was in this tiny prison-of-a-box. It was the devil's fault—and the warden's, of course.

Chapter 16

Nickolai knew Satan was angry with him for his faithfulness under persecution and his desire to keep the Sabbath. He was angry with Nickolai for all he had done as a pastor to help spread the gospel. The evil one was frustrated with the way the church had been growing under Nickolai's leadership in Kiev and the surrounding towns of the Ukraine. Could anyone be surprised that Satan would do everything in his power to stop the work?

It was Satan who had incited the KGB to persecute Nickolai when he lived in Kiev. Satan had sent Nickolai to the Siberian tundra as a prisoner to be isolated for a very long time—the rest of his life maybe. And now he was making life even harder for Nickolai by imprisoning him in a small box where there wasn't even room enough for him to stretch his legs.

But it didn't matter. None of it mattered just now. Nickolai would serve his time in the box for the sake of the gospel. How many more times he was going to have to do this was anybody's guess. He hoped this would be his last, but Nickolai knew he was only fooling himself if he really believed that. The warden was angry and offended that nothing he did or said had worked to change Nickolai's mind and make him obey orders. He despised Nickolai's stubbornness, and Nickolai was going to have to pay the price for it.

However, if Nickolai was going to be stubborn about something, he wanted to be stubborn for the gospel of Jesus. He determined in his mind that he would outlast the best and the worst of what the warden could give him. And he would do it gladly.

As morning turned into afternoon and afternoon into early evening, Nickolai again consoled himself by praying and quoting Scripture. As the darkness of night descended upon the stable, Nickolai could feel the stiffness slowly but surely returning to his joints. He tried to keep his knees moving. He also decided to sing to lift his spirits. He didn't have much of a singing voice, but the words to a familiar hymn came to mind.

"Under His wings I am safely abiding, though the night deepens and tempests are wild." The words were unsteady at first, but then Nickolai's voice grew stronger. "Still I can trust Him I know He will keep me, He has redeemed me and I am His child." Nickolai's voice swelled even fuller on the chorus line.

"Under His wings, under His wings, who from His love can sever? Under His wings my soul shall abide, safely abide forever."

The words worked like a tonic, and Nickolai realized that they were the magic he needed to keep his spirits up. In fact all through that first night when he awoke to try and bend his stiffening knees, he would hum a few lines of the hymn. "Under His wings, under His wings..." and then he would doze off into a surprisingly restful sleep.

Of course when he awakened the next morning it took him some time before he could get the circulation going in his legs again.

All that day and the following night he remembered his promise to himself and to God. Over and over again he reminded himself that he was determined to be true to his beliefs. He would endure the discomfort of persecution for Jesus' sake, no matter what the price. He would manage the pain by praying and quoting Bible promises and singing hymns whenever he needed a spiritual boost.

The pain grew unbearable after only two days, but Nickolai's courage remained strong. He spent his time recounting the blessings God had given him and the good memories he had of his family and church back home.

The routine was the same. In the morning Nickolai would watch through the cracks of the box as Oleg came to take Maksim to work for the day. At night he would watch them return, tired after their many trips to the spring, a kilometer away. Nickolai grew accustomed to the sound of the ox munching the sedge grass and his even breathing when he slept. It was a comfort to have another living creature near him—one that perhaps understood what it was like to be a prisoner against his will.

One thing was different this time around; Yuri made it a habit to bring Nickolai a can of water and a chunk of Russian black bread once a day. That was it, but it was better than nothing, and Nickolai was pretty sure that the bread was being brought in secret. He had detected a note of sympathy on Yuri's part, but he was sure the guard would never admit it.

If the warden shared any of Yuri's sentiments, he hid them well. Whatever scars there were that made the warden who he was, ran deep, and Nickolai felt badly for the man.

About noon on the tenth day, the lid to the box opened again. Again the fresh air and light was a shock to him, and again it was the face of the guard he saw first.

Yuri held a handkerchief over his nose and mouth as he shook his head disgustedly. "I don't understand you, preacher man," he said in a muffled tone, "and I probably never will!"

Again Yuri left Nickolai lying on the floor of the stable. Again Nickolai half crawled, half clawed his way to a pile of straw in the corner. The painful relief of being able to stretch his legs was excruciating, but Nickolai understood the pain this time around. He was getting used to the feeling of the box. He was ahead of the game this time.

Near dark Oleg returned to the stable with Maksim. When he had unhitched old Maksim, the ox came into the stable of his own accord. After all, it was his home. He paused as he walked past Nickolai and sniffed the smelly creature lying in the bed of straw.

Nickolai watched the ox eat his supper and then lie down in the soft straw beside him. Several times Nickolai thought he might attempt to crawl back to the barracks, but every time he tried to get to his knees, he would slump back onto the straw in pain. He was just too weak to even make it to the stable door, let alone all the way to the barracks.

But it didn't matter to Nickolai. He had nothing to lose one way or the other. In fact, sleeping next to Maksim's warm body was an advantage during the cooler nights.

As Nickolai dozed into a sleep of total exhaustion, he once again feebly hummed the familiar words, "safely abide forever."

CHAPTER 17

The next day Nickolai managed to get to his feet and limp back to the barracks. He couldn't go to the mess hall to eat, but Yuri brought him some borsch and Russian black bread.

Nickolai tried to thank the guard, but Yuri waved off the gesture as though he didn't want to hear it.

By Wednesday afternoon Nickolai thought he could probably work some if he didn't have to lift anything heavy or walk too much. No one was following him around to see that he worked, but he felt that it would be some kind of a statement to the warden if he could get in a few hours of work before sunset Wednesday.

The week was half over, and Sabbath was looming on his weekly horizon. It would come and when it did he had a feeling that the warden would put him back in the box. It was a battle of wills now between him and the warden. It appeared that the warden wanted to win this standoff at all costs, and if he couldn't, he was certainly going to make it a painful experience for Nickolai.

But pain or not, Nickolai also wanted to win this war that had now become one of government force versus allegiance to God.

Nickolai did work some on Wednesday, and then a full day on Thursday and Friday. By now he was beginning to get some real looks from the other prisoners. Everyone knew he was completely devoted to his God, but Nickolai was sure many of them had no real idea what sitting in a wooden box for ten days at a time had to do with it. Was he a religious fanatic? A lunatic? Was he a political prisoner just trying to make a political statement?

Sooner or later Nickolai knew he was going to get an opportunity to share his story. Sooner or later someone would come asking, and Nickolai would get a chance to tell them why he was so devoted to serving his God. But for now the others just watched and wondered at Nickolai's vigilant faith.

And when the Sabbath day arrived, things turned out exactly as Nickolai knew they would. He was put back in the box.

It amazed him that the warden was sticking to this strategy of discipline. Every time he put Nickolai in the box, Nickolai was out of commission for ten days, and then it took at least a day for him to recover and recoup his strength. That left him only two days to resume work again before being put back into the box. If the warden wanted to run an efficient camp, locking Nickolai up for such lengthy periods of time wasn't working. At least not if he wanted to get any work out of Nickolai.

The whole thing didn't make much sense, but then the whole strategy of the soviet government didn't make much sense to Nickolai, either. Why force a person or group of people to give up something they cherished? The whole thing was like trying to force a man to turn against his own family, but of course the prison warden wouldn't care about that. He had no religion. He would never comprehend the strength of Nickolai's allegiance to his God and his church family. If he had, he would have never persisted in fighting against Nickolai's incredible, immovable devotion to the service of his God.

And so it went as the short summer weeks turned into the chill of autumn. Frost came in August and then a light snow in early September. While in the box, Nickolai could not afford to sleep for very long periods of time. Every few minutes he had to wake up to move his legs and arms so he could keep the circulation going.

When the frigid days of winter came in late October, Nickolai worried. How would he stay alive? How would he manage to stay warm all cooped up in a small box?

Nickolai wasn't sure it really mattered anymore. If he perished, he perished. If it was time for him to lay down his life for Jesus, then he was at peace with such a fate.

But just as resigned as he was to this possibility, he was just as sure that God had a plan for his life—something in store for him as God's witness, though it be in a box.

It was at times like this that the scriptures became Nickolai's greatest comfort. His favorite passages were Psalms 23, 91, and 140. These wonderful chapters helped him focus on the real battle that was raging—the battle between good and evil.

Yuri must have been feeling sorry for Nickolai again, because one morning when he brought the preacher his bread and water, he also brought two thick blankets. It had been an especially cold night, and the gesture warmed Nickolai's heart with gratefulness to Yuri and God. The blankets wouldn't keep him toasty, but they would take the edge off the cold winter nights.

All the water in camp was freezing over by now. Even the barrels of water brought from the spring on a daily basis would freeze by morning. During the early days of winter, Petya, the cook, would break the thick sheet of ice at the top of each barrel in the mornings. But when the real temperatures of winter settled in and dropped to zero and below, the water froze solid in a matter of hours. Petya began having Oleg bring the barrels inside the kitchen.

Because of the extreme temperature, Nickolai knew he couldn't afford to let the water get chilled. If he allowed the water to start to freeze, it would drop his body temperature even further when he drank it. From now on he knew he would have to drink right away when Yuri brought him his can of water.

The hours of daylight were few now, and the nights longer. Nickolai's breath made puffs of steam when he breathed, and when he pulled the blanket up around his face a crust of frost quickly gathered. How he managed to stay warm in the ice-cold temperatures, he never knew, but one thing was sure—with God all things are possible. He was Nickolai's ever-present help in trouble.

Chapter 18

L ate one afternoon Yuri came into the stable quite unexpectedly. He pushed and pulled Nickolai's wooden crate to a dark corner of the stable away from the doorway and the chilly winds that sometimes blew in when the door was open.

Nickolai was surprised at the ease with which Yuri moved the box, but then he realized that he was not the stout man he once was. Even through his coat he could feel his ribs. When Yuri began forking hay up around the crate, Nickolai's heart was touched. The hay would do wonders to insulate him against the cold winter air. Now, beyond a shadow of a doubt, he knew the guard really did care what happened to him.

"Thank you," was all Nickolai said, but the two of them knew what such a gesture could truly mean to Nickolai. It would very likely save his life.

Nickolai was sure that Yuri was acting on his own and that the warden knew nothing of Yuri's thoughtful deeds. The food he had brought, the water, the blankets, and the hay piled high around his box—all were simple acts of kindness, and yet ones that couldn't be misconstrued.

The cold days of winter turned to a wet spring. Unable to move about in the box when he was imprisoned there, the damp air chilled Nickolai to the bone. He wasn't sure which was worse—the frigid, mind-numbing days of winter, or the wet bone-chilling days of spring.

When summer finally came, and his ten-day confinements in the crate continued, the insects returned and so did the memories of his first days in the box. Again his skin swelled up from the bites of mosquitoes, black flies, and no-see-ums. Surprisingly, in spite of the moderate temperatures outside, many days in the stable under the tin roof turned oppressively warm. This brought problems again with cleanliness since Nickolai was not allowed out of the box to go to the bathroom. And of course this just made the fly problem even worse.

All that summer Nickolai endured the sessions of being confined in the wooden box. All that summer he would approach the Sabbath with stubborn faithfulness and a tenacity that impressed even the warden. If Nickolai could have seen how it really affected the warden, he would have been greatly encouraged.

Nevertheless, the warden would not give in, and back Nickolai would go to the box each Sabbath. He would endure his 10-day sentence, be released, and then suffer great anguish as he worked to regain the use of his legs. Then he would spend a couple of days working with Vadeem on camp repairs and projects before being locked up again in the box.

As fall arrived and once again stretched into winter, Nickolai became known as the preacher in the box. He hated to think that his time in the box was being wasted, and some days he had to wonder what in the world God's long-range plan might be. He had heard of saints who suffered in prison for 20 and 30 years, and he dreaded the possibility of such a fate, but even that didn't seem to deter him much anymore. It seemed to be part of Nickolai's routine now, a part of who he was and who he had become.

Most days he wasn't sure which would be better—to live another day and suffer the slow painful deterioration of his body through such torture, or experience a quick death that would end his earthly life.

But again it didn't really matter. Hadn't his life already been one long trial of persecution for the sake of the gospel? Why question God's plan now. Nickolai truly did trust his heavenly Father. Some day all would be clear. In the meantime he tried not to ask too many philosophical questions about the quality of life or about God's overall plan for him. He just kept quoting scriptures that promised answers someday, and this gave him simple strength to endure for yet another day.

"All things work together for good to those who love God, to those who are called according to His purpose," he would recite to himself countless times while in the box.

All the verses he had memorized in his life were coming back to him now, and they were a real source of comfort in his time of need.

"Do not fear any of those things that you are about to suffer. Indeed, the devil is about to throw some of you into prison, that you may be tested, and you will have tribulation ten days." This part of the verse always made Nickolai smile ironically. He knew the verse was more symbolic than literal—but still it was satisfying to think that John the Revelator had used the very number of days in the prophecy that matched the number of days Nickolai was having to suffer each time in the box.

"Be faithful until death, and I will give you a crown of life." That was the part of the passage that always gave him the greatest hope. It reminded him that nothing really mattered in life except that he remain faithful to Jesus.

And so to witness for God in a communist prison was truly a privilege. As far as Nickolai could tell, there were no Christians in the camp. He could hardly believe that, but as of yet, none had shone their true colors or dared to come forward even if just to encourage him.

But if his witness for Jesus could bring even one soul to Christ, he felt it would be worth it. All the pain and hardship he had endured would stand for something—it would not be for nothing. And who knew? If one man were brought to Jesus, maybe others would follow.

Another cold winter followed on the heels of autumn, and then spring edged its way into camp. One spring day when Nickolai was once again pulled from the box, he lay there in the straw looking out through the stable doorway. The month of May had come, and although this time of year was still quite cool, the sunshine and clear blue sky warmed his heart.

As Nickolai slowly flexed his legs, trying to get the kinks out of his knees, he thanked God for life. He thanked Jesus for the chance to be a living witness for Christ instead of being a martyr. It was amazing that he could endure such hardship and not resent the leading of his heavenly Father, but it was famous lines from Scripture that always kept him upbeat in his attitude toward life. One of his favorites was from the writings of Paul.

"For I have learned in whatever state I am, to be content."

And that of course was what always made the difference. How could it not? Nickolai had given his life totally to God, and God was giving him just what he needed day by day until the time was right to reveal the next phase of His divine plan.

CHAPTER 19

A few weeks later unusual guests showed up at the prison camp. Three military officers rode in on horses, and it was obvious by their appearance that one of them was a high-ranking colonel in the army—all the way from Nizhniy Novgorod.

It soon became clear that they were there to inspect the camp. The warden pulled out all the stops and made quite a show of things—not that he had anything remarkable to brag about at the prison camp. It was a standard camp out in the middle of nowhere on the Siberian steppes, housing some 300 prisoners with no notorious or political criminals among them.

But guests at the camp were rare, so giving these special visitors a tour was the biggest thing that had happened at the camp in years. They were shown the officers' quarters, the kitchen and mess hall, and the barracks. Nickolai could hear their conversation as the tour took them near the stables.

"What's in here?" the colonel asked, pointing at the low-roofed shed where Nickolai's box was kept.

The warden glanced through the open doorway of the stable. He had put Nickolai in the box just three days ago, but he had hoped to avoid having to explain the situation to the colonel.

"Oh, this is where we house the worst prisoners," he said nonchalantly. "Severe punishment keeps the insubordinate ones under control."

"Why types of punishment?"

"Oh, various types." The warden squirmed.

The officer stepped through the doorway and peered into the dim shadows of the stable.

"We keep them locked up in boxes like that one." The warden pointed at Nickolai's wooden crate in the corner.

"How many prisoners are locked up right now?" The officer was painfully persistent, and Nickolai could sense the uneasiness in the warden's voice.

"Well, we only have one man in here right now."

"And he's in for what, specifically?"

"For refusing to carry out his duties."

The officer stepped closer to the wooden crate, but immediately stepped back as his nose caught a whiff of the foul stench coming from the crate.

"Whew!" he exclaimed. "And how long have you been punishing him for this sort of insubordination?"

"Mmmm," the warden scratched his head. "Only three days this time, so far, but he's in for a ten-day stint."

"A ten-day stint?" the colonel looked skeptical. "And you say he won't work? How many times has he been insubordinate?"

"Well—now—he's been giving us trouble ever since he arrived in camp." The warden's eyes darted back and forth between the box and the colonel. "Every time we let him out, he disobeys again, so we just put him back in the box."

The colonel looked at the box again. "And you've tried this how many times?"

"Hmmm—I guess—uh, we've been doing it for pretty close to two years now."

The colonel looked at the warden incredulously, his mouth dropping open in disbelief.

Through the cracks in the crate Nickolai watched the whole thing transpire, and with bated breath, he waited for the conversation to continue. It was becoming more and more apparent that the colonel did not approve of such crude forms of treatment, and it also appeared as though the warden was about to get reprimanded for it.

"Two years?"

"Yes, sir."

"You've had this man locked up in this tiny box for ten-day stints repeatedly during the last two years! That must be some—forty or fifty times at least!"

The warden looked embarrassed. He paused, and then finally replied, "Well, yes, I'd say that's about right."

"Do you mean to tell me that you've been locking this man up in this crate for two years, and it hasn't done any good? Even with this type of punishment, he's still being disobedient, or insubordinate, or whatever you want to call it!" the colonel was getting more irritated by the minute. "Did it ever occur to you, officer, that there may be a good reason why this man isn't following your orders! I mean, two years, and he still hasn't come around!"

The warden looked shocked and bewildered and aghast all in the same instant.

"Well, did you?"

"No—no, sir! It didn't occur to me just like that—but now that you put it that way, it does sound pretty ridiculous!"

"Ridiculous!" the colonel almost shouted. "I'll say it sounds ridiculous! Totally idiotic, if you ask me! In fact, I'm beginning to question who the intelligent one is around here! Certainly not you!" he continued to glare at the warden. "I ought to have your commission revoked for running such an operation! This isn't discipline! It's just plain torture! We Russians officers may be tough and mean as wildcats, but we're not animals!"

CHAPTER 20

The colonel abruptly turned back to the crate. "Open the box!" he ordered, his voice still livid with anger. "Open the box at once!"

SDO-3

Yuri came forward and opened the lock that held the latch. He lifted the lid and reached into the box to help Nickolai stand to his feet.

It had only been three days since Nickolai had been put into the box, but by now his legs were already like rubber. He tried to stand without wavering, but he couldn't. The strength was just not there. With so few days between the stints in the box, he had slowly lost the ability to recuperate quickly and each time his legs would atrophy a little more.

"Here! Lay him in this pile of straw over here!" the colonel barked. "And get him a drink of water!" He waved his hand to ward off the flies and the stench that was permeating the shed.

"And bring a bucket of water so he can clean himself up!" The colonel turned to Nickolai and shook his head again. "What's your name, young man?"

"Panchuk, sir. Nickolai Panchuk."

The officer continued looking kindly at Nickolai. "Is it true what the warden says? That you won't work."

"No. It's not true," Nickolai swallowed some of the water from the cup Yuri handed him. "I will work. I'll work harder than all the other prisoners, if need be. I'll get up early and stay up late every night, but—but I can't dishonor God and work on His holy Sabbath day."

The colonel raised his eyebrows.

"The seventh day of every week is God's Subota," Nickolai continued, seeing the opportunity to witness once again about his beloved Sabbath. "I was raised to keep it holy, and I can't violate my conscience, sir! On the seventh day of each week I can't work because it would be disobeying the commands of my God."

Nickolai wanted to be respectful of the officer, but right now he was lying in a pile of straw. It was hard to stand at attention or salute the colonel while lying prostrate on the stable floor. The nervousness showed on his face.

"At ease, prisoner," came the colonel's reassuring command as he stared down at Nickolai. "What did you do for a living before you came to this camp?"

"I was a pastor, sir. It's why I was sent here in the first place—because I wouldn't turn over a list of my church members to the KGB." Nickolai's voice wavered and then almost broke with emotion as he added, "I could not, sir! It would have betrayed the confidence my members had placed in me as their spiritual leader."

Nickolai felt strange. Why was he baring his soul to this unknown army officer? He felt chagrined and relieved at the same time. He couldn't explain it, but somehow it seemed the right thing to do at this point.

"So you will work, but you won't work on Saturdays? Your Subota as you call it."

"Yes, sir. I'll work hard, before sunup and well after dark, to make up for the time I miss on Saturdays."

The colonel looked at the warden. "Do you have a job like this? One that can be done on some days and not others? A job that can be done in fewer days if this man works more hours each of the other days?"

The warden thought for a long moment. "Well, there is the water that needs to be brought from the spring a kilometer away." He glanced at the colonel. "We need barrels of water, and it usually takes a man and ox seven days of hauling to bring enough water for the camp. Enough for drinking water, cooking, and any washing the men need to do."

The warden looked at Nickolai lying in the straw and then at the colonel. "I suppose we could give that a try. The man doing it now works from dawn to dusk and barely has time enough to bring the nine or ten barrels of water we need on average per day. If Panchuk wants to get up and work before dawn each day and then work after dark, maybe he can manage to bring enough by Friday night. I doubt it, but we can give it a try." The warden had a cynical look in his eye, but he chose his words carefully in front of the colonel.

The officer brightened. "All right, then, Panchuk. It's a deal. Let's see what you can do. Tomorrow is Tuesday. The warden says that if you can bring enough water by Friday night, you can have your day off. Five days of work in four. If you can do it, then Saturday is a free day."

And then the colonel got a serious look in his eye as he looked straight at Nickolai. "But if you can't keep up your end of the bargain, you're going to have to haul water on Saturdays, too. Your Subota, as you call it. Are we clear on this?"

"Absolutely."

"I'm curious, Panchuk." The colonel searched Nickolai's face—although it was filled with pain, it held the peace of heaven.

"You have been so stubborn in refusing to work on your Subota," he continued. "What happens if Saturday comes and you still don't have enough water? We've got a deal and yet somehow I get the feeling that you would probably still choose to go into the box than work and violate your holy day."

Nickolai thought about the question before answering the kindest Russian military officer he had ever met. He chose his words carefully because he wanted to honor the colonel's faith in him, and the warden's willingness to give him a chance to prove himself.

"If I honor my God, He will honor me, sir. He knows I wish to worship Him in prayer and quiet meditation on that day, so I am placing my confidence in Him, that He will give me the strength to complete the challenge. I will work half the night, if need be, just to complete my part of the bargain and secure for myself the right to worship my God on that day."

"You know, I believe you will," the colonel nodded and smiled kindly. The man's generosity made Nickolai feel warm inside, and it gave him hope that everything would turn out for the best after all. It seemed that this was the break he had been hoping for, the chance he had been wanting for two years—a chance to show everyone the sovereignty of his God.

Nickolai rested the remainder of the day, trying to limber up and get his knees to work again. By nightfall he felt pretty good; however, as he lay on his bunk that night in the barracks, he thought about the distance to the spring. It had to be about a kilometer. Maybe a little more. That would be almost three kilometers each round trip. Nickolai figured it would take maybe two and a half to three hours for each load of water.

From what he had seen, the oxcart carried two barrels at a time, so that meant he needed to haul five loads a day to bring the quota of water per day. But he needed to haul enough water for Saturday's supply too. There was no question about it—Nickolai knew he was going to have to haul at least one or two extra loads a day to make it!

With his mind whirling, he took time to pray before dozing off. *Lord, help me not to worry. Help me to have the energy I need to take on this amazing challenge. It is truly a challenge straight from the courts of heaven.*

CHAPTER 21

Before dawn had even lit the eastern sky the next morning, Nickolai was out at the stables helping Oleg the ox cart driver hitch up old Maksim. Oleg would be working with Nickolai for the day to teach him the routine of hauling water from the spring.

Nickolai knew that this was his chance to win Sabbath privileges and be a powerful witness for God. For two years now he had been confined repeatedly in a wooden box for ten days at a time because he wouldn't work on the Sabbath. But he had remained true to his convictions and suffered everything the warden could throw at him.

Now God had provided Nickolai a way of escape from the torture box with his faith still intact. It was time for Nickolai to witness in a different sort of way.

There was so much at stake. Would God help Nickolai to do what seemed to be an impossibility? Could Nickolai and Maksim haul seven days' worth of water in just six days of work each week? And this week the task was even more daunting—five days worth of water in four.

In Nickolai's mind it would take a miracle, but that was, of course, what God was all about. It was what Nickolai's busy life as a pastor had been all about. It was what his interrogation episodes with the KGB had been about, his eventual sentence at this prison camp, and his confinement in the box for refusing to work on the Sabbath day. And it was what his release and new assignment with Maksim were all about. Nickolai's life of sacrifice and service to God had been one miracle after another, and Nickolai doubted that the miracles would stop now. There was too much at stake.

And so it was that Nickolai and Oleg set out for the spring across the treeless steppes. It took them more than an hour to make the trek as they walked along laboriously behind the plodding ox.

"Can't we make this old ox hurry any faster!" Nickolai complained as the oxcart lumbered slowly along past muskegs and around bogs. "If he walks this slow all day, we'll never get our five loads in by the end of today!"

"Oh, we'll get the water in, all right, but old Maksim has never promised me that we'd do it before dark. Often we come trudging in long after dark. You should know that! You were there in the shed to witness it lots of times!"

Nickolai stared at Oleg, a stunned look settling in on his face. If they couldn't manage the regular number of loads in a given day, how were they going to be able to get the extra barrels of water hauled to camp?

Oleg just shook his head. "I guess you thought this was going to be an easy job!" he snorted.

"Uh, no, not actually, but I was hoping we would be able to get Maksim to move along a little faster."

Oleg made a face, and shook his head again. "Look! I'm sorry that you had to stay cooped up in that box, and I'm glad the colonel let you out, but this business of getting more barrels of water so you can have your day off is crazy. Old Maksim here knows nothing about any of that. All he knows is that when he wants to walk, he walks. And when he wants to walk slower, there's nothing you can do to hurry him up!"

Nickolai wanted to say something, but he didn't.

"I know what you're thinking!" Oleg kept on. "You were thinking that since you're a preacher man, your God would work some kind of miracle! I'm right, aren't I?" Oleg gave the ox a slap on his rump.

"You thought your God would reach down out of the sky above and tickle old Maksim's ear or something to make him move faster, didn't you! And then Maksim would run like nobody's business and have all the water for the week hauled to the camp in six days! Hey! Maybe even in five?"

Oleg was still shaking his head. His reaction seemed logical enough. Should Nickolai have expected anything less? He had thought that the other prisoners might admire him for standing up for what he believed in, but maybe that wasn't the case at all. Maybe they had no respect for a man who wouldn't work, especially if he was asking for one day of work off in seven? All the men were working hard, and they were all being held at this prison camp against their will. Then too, like the warden, they didn't know a thing about Nickolai's God or the devotion he had for his Maker.

Nickolai had nothing more to say, so he walked the remainder of the distance in silence. What was the use?

The first rays of sunshine were just beginning to peak over the horizon when they arrived at the spring. Nickolai helped Oleg dip wooden buckets into the pool of water at the spring and then pour them into the barrels waiting on the oxcart.

It wasn't a hard task, but several times Nickolai sloshed water from the buckets on himself. The morning air was still chilly, and the cold water made Nickolai shiver. He realized that if he wanted to stay dry he was going to have to learn how to put more water into the barrels and less on himself. Besides, if he were careless, it would take that much longer to fill the barrels.

Oleg put the wooden lids on the two barrels and then nudged Maksim forward with his ox goad. Nickolai was glad to see that Oleg no longer used his leather prod to beat Maksim. He used the goad instead to guide the ox and send him signals as to what he wanted him to do.

The trip back to camp took even longer since the cart was loaded down with full barrels of water. Several times Nickolai tried to urge

Maksim along faster, but always the old ox resisted his efforts. In fact, any attempts to hurry him along seemed to make him move slower.

If Nickolai could have gotten into the harness to help Maksim pull the cart along faster, he thought he would gladly do it. As it was, he and Oleg were at the mercy of Maksim and his whims to move along at his own pace. In the end Nickolai realized Oleg was right—there was nothing they could do but walk along patiently beside the cart.

CHAPTER 22

At the camp they worked to unload the barrels from the cart, trying to avoid spilling any of the precious water. It was a simple routine, but Nickolai wanted to get on the road again. Unfortunately, as they began the process all over again, neither Maksim, nor Oleg seemed in any hurry to move at a pace that suited Nickolai.

By now Nickolai was beginning to feel that he would rather work by himself than have Oleg along. In fact, he was sure of it. As the two of them filled the barrels for the second time and then turned old Maksim around for the trip back to camp, Nickolai began to form a plan.

Why tie up the time of two men doing a job that could be done by one? The job was turning out to be much easier than Nickolai had anticipated. Old Maksim was doing most of the work anyway.

Nickolai waited to speak his mind until after they had unloaded the two barrels of water at the kitchen.

"I've been thinking," Nickolai ventured. "It's a long way out to the spring, and it seems a terrible waste of manpower to have us both walking all the way out there. You've taught me what I need to know, and now the rest is up to Maksim. Why don't you let me try a run by myself? If I have any trouble, I can let you know when I get back."

Nickolai wiped the sweat from his forehead with his sleeve and ran his hand through his hair. "Do you think that would work?"

"Hmmm—you're probably right," Oleg admitted as he stared at the empty water barrels they had just loaded on the cart. He stole a glance at Nickolai. "You'll probably have no trouble."

And so Nickolai began his new job, solo, and he put his energy into it. As soon as he was out of earshot, he began to do his best to get Maksim to increase his speed. But old Maksim didn't appreciate being hurried along. A few times Nickolai tried whipping him up a bit with the goad, but after a few hundred meters of this, old Maksim slowed his pace down to almost a standstill.

In the end Nickolai realized once again the truth of what Oleg had said—old Maksim just couldn't be made to run faster. He would walk when he wanted to, and he would stop when he wanted to. And short of beating the ox mercilessly, it wasn't going to change things any.

They made several more trips out to the spring, but as the day wound down, so did Maksim's energy. Near the end he was walking slower and slower. Now Nickolai was really frustrated, and if the whole thing hadn't been so pathetic, he might have laughed.

To Nickolai it was obvious that Maksim didn't care how many loads he could get in before dark. He was just an animal. But animal or not, in some ways it appeared that Maksim was just another one of the prisoners. He was being forced to work against his will—harnessed to a cart every morning and made to walk back and forth all day to the spring. That was the life of a prisoner in a prison camp, wasn't it? Work, work, work.

Like machines, Nickolai and Maksim would spend each day working as though that was what they had been made to do. They might not like it, but they would do it anyway, because that was what everyone did out here on the windswept steppes of Siberia.

But all of that was just rhetoric. At the end of each day, Nickolai needed to have more than his quota of five cartloads of water in camp—by the end of the week he needed ten extra barrels of water or he was going to have to go through more pain and alienation in the box. This was his one chance! This was the opportunity Nickolai had been longing for during the two years he had been cooped up in the wooden crate.

So whether Maksim felt like moving fast, or not, they needed to get that extra water in by Friday evening. If they had to haul water half the night, they were going to do it. Nickolai was going to prove to the warden that working hard and having a Sabbath day's rest was possible. He wanted Yuri to know it, and Oleg, and any other person in camp who witnessed his persistent loyalty to the Sabbath and his God.

But by the time the shadows were long on the Siberian landscape, Nickolai knew it wasn't enough. He was going to have to work after dark. The sun was low in the sky as the fifth cartload rumbled into camp, and he knew he needed at least one more load tonight if he was going to make a dent in the ten extra barrels he needed by Friday night.

When Nickolai had finished unloading the barrels, he turned the cart around quickly and headed out of camp for one more trip to the spring. But Maksim had other ideas. He pulled the cart off the road and toward the stables just forty or fifty meters away. Not to be outdone, Nickolai pulled hard to the left to steer Maksim back onto the road.

It was a battle of man against beast, brain against brute. Maksim wasn't used to going back out to the spring this time of night, but Nickolai knew they had to have that extra load of water. Nickolai used the goad to persuade Maksim.

"Can't you get it into your thick skull that I'm doing this for your own good!" Nickolai half shouted. "I'm just as tired as you are," he added with a stubborn resolution that surprised even himself, "but it doesn't matter! We're going to do this whether we like it, or not!"

Nickolai felt bad yelling at Maksim like that. The old ox was tired. He had worked all day pulling that cart back and forth from the spring. They had already hauled five loads of water and walked what Nickolai figured was about 14 or 15 kilometers. And now they were going to walk maybe three more kilometers, and put in another two to three hours of work.

He wished that he could somehow convey the idea to Maksim that a day of rest for the man on Sabbath would be a day of rest for the ox.

But he guessed that he would have to leave that job up to God. Only the Creator of man and beast truly knew how to do that.

CHAPTER 23

The next morning Nickolai was up before everyone. He was up before any of the prisoners had stirred, and before the warden or guards. He was up before even the cook had begun to stoke the fires in the kitchen. But the sun was already peeking over the horizon, and Nickolai guessed it must be about 4:00 a.m.

He was a little weary from the short night, and his legs were a bit stiff, but he flexed them again and again to limber them up. He couldn't afford to sleep in or slack off now. He needed to be up and going, out on that road to the spring so he could get enough water barrels hauled in by Friday.

The sun wasn't up yet. It hadn't even begun to rise in the east as Nickolai threw on his clothes, grabbed a flask of water, and went to the stables to rouse old Maksim. Of course the hour was earlier than Maksim was accustomed to, but Nickolai managed to get him on his feet and into his harness.

The old ox eyed Nickolai warily as if he were suspicious of the man's every move. And why shouldn't he be? This man was crazy! Urging him to hurry all day long, pushing him to work all hours of the night, and now he was getting the ox up and out of the stable at an unearthly hour.

Nickolai was in a hurry to get going. He didn't think he had time to eat a regular breakfast, but he did stop by the kitchen for a carryout meal. The cook was up by now and gave him some bread and carrots to take with him. Nickolai knew he could stop by the kitchen later that morning for some hot borsch and Russian bread, but for now the cold food would have to do.

The man and ox headed west out of the camp and toward the spring. Maksim knew the way even in the dark. He could walk the distance himself without anyone guiding him—he would have even been able to make the trip with Nickolai sleeping in the back of the oxcart. Unfortunately, there wasn't room in the cart. The barrels were too big and took up all the space.

The morning was peaceful at this hour with the silence of nature all around them. The only sound that broke the stillness of the morning was the creaking of old Maksim's harness and the squeaking wheels on the oxcart. Other than that there was little to punctuate the early morning hour.

In the pale light of pre-dawn, Nickolai could see a few lemmings come out of the burrows they had made for themselves in the matted sedge grass lining the roadway. A little further along he saw a snowy owl perched on a craggy rock poking its way through the Siberian landscape. And of course there were the snowshoe hares now brown with their summer camouflage.

At one point Nickolai rounded a bend in the road and suddenly caught his breath. Sitting in the middle of the road was a large wolf, his lanky body, tall and lean—Nickolai guessed he was about three feet tall at the shoulder. And he just sat there staring at the man and ox.

Maksim pulled to a stop for a few tense moments. It was obvious the ox didn't really know what to do. Nickolai sensed he was frightened, because he could see the muscles ripple and tighten in the ox's neck and shoulders.

Did Nickolai need to worry? Was this wolf out scouting for a meal? Would he come back with others from his wolf pack? The wolf finally got up and trotted off to the north. Nickolai breathed a little easier after the wolf left. No one had alerted him to the possibility of wolf attacks out here, and he and Oleg hadn't encountered the wolf the previous day.

He consoled himself with the idea that the wolf was probably not a threat to them anyway. There were plenty of lemmings and snowshoe hares for the wolf to hunt and eat. Of course, when the harsh winter struck Siberia come October, Nickolai was not sure where he and the ox would rank on the food chain for a hungry pack of wolves.

Food was not exactly abundant for either man or beast in this deserted country. The only other sizeable game on the steppes of Siberia would be reindeer that traveled in scattered herds. Or so he had been told when he asked Petya, the cook, during a conversation with him in the kitchen one evening.

CHAPTER 24

It had been on one of those days months back when Nickolai had just gotten out of the box and was trying to recuperate. He had managed to hobble to the kitchen late in the day to get something to eat. After the evening meal, he had stayed late and helped Petya scrub the pots and pans and prepare some sour dough for baking the next morning.

They worked in silence until Petya began talking about cooking and the limited supply of ingredients he had in the camp. He was hoping for some reindeer meat that winter.

"The reindeer herds come this way some years—other years we never see them," Petya had said as he covered the sour dough with a towel and set it aside. "When they do come, and we can shoot a few, we lay aside enough meat for a good long while. Fifteen or 20 reindeer is a lot of meat, but of course it doesn't go far with 300 men in camp."

Petya glanced at Nickolai and raised his eyebrows. "I suppose you're wondering where the guns are that they use to hunt the reindeer."

"Well, I hadn't thought of that, but now that you mention it, I guess, I haven't seen any guns in camp."

"That's because they don't bring the guns out unless the reindeer herds come this way. I think they must keep the rifles locked up in the warden's office, or something. No one really knows. I've never been told." He continued, "Of course they only give the rifles to the guards, but no one really gives it much thought. Everyone is just glad to get some meat to eat—reindeer meat is pretty good eating."

Petya began to hang the pots and pans up to dry, and Nickolai did what he could to help. "If the reindeer don't come this way, then we have to satisfy ourselves with the cabbage, turnips, beets, and onions we grow in our gardens. They keep pretty well, and in cold weather we can store them underground in beds of hay."

Nickolai thought about the vegetables that Petya cooked up in the borsch—cabbage and beets mostly. Borsch was something every Russian ate every day. To not have borsch for a main meal was considered almost unthinkable.

Petya had big forearms from his work in the kitchen. Making bread, cutting up turnips and beets, and scrubbing pots and pans could do that to you. He was a quiet man and didn't appear to have many friends. But he was a great cook—everybody said so.

"You're a good cook, Petya," Nicholai found himself saying, "especially with the limited resources you have to work with."

"You just say that because you don't know any better," Petya insisted, laughing good-naturedly, and Nickolai found himself laughing too. "You've been locked up in the box too long. You're always hungry and anything that hits your tongue tastes good to you," Petya added.

Nickolai's reminiscing ended when he reached the spring. As he filled the water barrels, the sun finally rose in all its glory. He worked quickly to finish the job, and then turned Maksim and the oxcart around. It felt like they were making progress, and Maksim was responding well to the urgency Nickolai felt.

At this pace Nickolai was sure they would be able to bring home six loads of water—twelve barrels. And who knew? Maybe they would be able to do even more than that. In Nickolai's mind seven trips to the spring was not out of the question.

All that morning Nickolai drove the ox hard, never letting up with the stick, never allowing the ox to rest or pause by the road for a little sedge grass. Today was Wednesday. If he could manage to get fourteen barrels of water into the camp by bedtime, and another fourteen on Thursday, he would only have to get ten on Friday. That would give him time to get home and prepare properly for the Sabbath when it was time for the sun to set.

But Nickolai was getting way ahead of himself, and he had misjudged the nature of a beast of burden. As morning turned to afternoon and the sun turned west, old Maksim began to slow his pace. His shoulders sagged a little more, and his tongue began to hang out when they stopped at the spring or at the camp to unload the full barrels. Of course Nickolai let the ox have a good long drink while he was filling the barrels at the spring. That was efficiency at its best. Why not give Maksim a chance to rest, and drink his fill while Nickolai was busy filling the water barrels?

But when they were back in camp, Nickolai paused only long enough for Petya to hand him some bread and a tin bowlful of red borsch. At these times, Nickolai never gave Maksim a chance to get more than a short drink.

And so they plodded on with Maksim growing more tired each hour and slower with each leg of each trip. By late afternoon it was obvious that pushing Maksim hard had sapped the ox's stamina and his willingness to keep going. In fact, the fifth trip to the spring took more than three hours. The sun was so low in the sky now that Nickolai could see they were going to be hard pressed to get six loads of water—they would have to work long after dark again to do it.

He was so frustrated with Maksim as the time slipped away, but what could he do? He determined that he would simply have to drive the ox harder! He had no other choice! They would have to go faster to get the water in by Sabbath! Nickolai had come too far in his plan to let it go now!

With a stronger resolve, Nickolai vowed to make Maksim work if it was the last thing he did on earth! But Nickolai knew that if this was going to really happen something was going to have to change! He was going to have to reshape the way Maksim did things. To modify an animal's behavior, you had to force him to obey, either by punishing him for wrong behavior or by rewarding him for obedience.

He cringed as he suddenly realized that this was exactly what the warden had been trying to do with him. The warden had been stubbornly putting him in the wooden crate trying to break him.

"Is that what I'm doing to you?" Nickolai asked incredulously as he stared at Maksim. "Is that what this is all about?"

The lemmings along the roadside stopped their squeaking and sat up to hear more of the debate. The snowshoe hares browsing on the short sedge grasses perked up their ears to hear the final verdict.

For a long moment, Nickolai gave the idea some thought, but then just as suddenly he snapped out of his reverie.

"There's no time for that now!" he argued, his mind seesawing back in the other direction. "I don't have time to be feeling sorry for an ox that doesn't want to work hard. If I can do it, then he can do it, too!"

Nickolai didn't let up. "I'll push you all day, Maksim, and all night if I need to! I'll go without meals—I'll go without sleep!"

In frustration he whacked Maksim on the rump with the goad, and the old ox jumped forward. Maksim was going to work hard all day every day—Nickolai would see to that!

Of course at the end of the week Maksim was going to get the Sabbath off just like Nickolai was. The pastor smiled in spite of his irritation. Any rest for Nickolai would be a rest for Maksim. The old ox didn't know it yet, but he would soon enough. Come Sabbath he would be lying in the stable enjoying the sedge grass piled high in his feeding trough.

CHAPTER 25

On Thursday morning Nickolai was up even earlier than the day before. But his worst fears from the day before had been realized—try as he might, he had managed to haul only six loads of water.

As he thought about how hard he had worked until long after dark, the whole thing was disheartening. What else did he need to do that he had not already done? Short of giving up, there seemed no answers.

When Nickolai went to the stables, Maksim seemed listless and tired, as though he had already used up the day's ration of energy. As they headed out of camp, the old ox walked with his head down and no light in his eyes. He didn't even look Nickolai's way when the man tried to give him his favorite snack—a carrot.

Nickolai knew he was now paying the price for pushing Maksim to the limit two days in a row. And in some sad sort of way it seemed only right. He had ignored the common sense logic and the goodness in his heart that said he should be kinder to the animal. Justice in nature's law of averages had prevailed, and Nickolai couldn't deny that it should be so.

Hour after hour the ox plodded slowly along with no sense of the urgency Nickolai felt. He had worked overtime two days in a row, and now it seemed that he was thinking he deserved to slow things down a bit. After all, it wasn't his neck on the line. Why should he work faster simply to trade one day for another? Of course he had no knowledge of Nickolai's Sabbath or the importance of the standoff between the preacher and the warden.

The sun passed its zenith as morning turned to afternoon. White cumulous clouds scudded across the landscape now green with the short grasses of summer growth. A few white cardamine flowers stared up at the man and ox as they passed by with the creaking water cart.

Suddenly the lone wolf came out to watch them again. This time he sat on a slight rise to the south, following their every move as though the man and beast were the best source of entertainment he had seen in days.

But Nickolai hardly noticed them. He was growing more and more discouraged by the hour. All his efforts to work hard and deliver the quota of barrels by sunset Friday were going to be to no avail. It just wasn't going to be enough. Nickolai could feel it in his bones. There wasn't enough time.

Nickolai filled the barrels for the third time that day, and then turned the cart around again. As he trudged along the road, Nickolai did the math one more time. Ten barrels of water per day were needed—fifty by Friday night so that he wouldn't have to haul any on the Sabbath. Two barrels of water per trip meant that he needed to make twenty-five trips in just four days.

With the six loads he hauled on Tuesday and the six on Wednesday, he would need a total of thirteen more. That meant he would need seven at least, for today, and then maybe six for Friday.

How was he going to be able to do it? He hadn't managed to bring in seven loads either of the other two days, and today Maksim was working even slower. Seven loads seemed impossible.

To be sure, at this rate they'd never make it by sundown Friday. If he had begun working on Sunday, maybe he would have been able to make one extra trip per day. Maybe then he could have gotten the number of barrels needed by Friday night.

By now old Maksim was even limping a bit, and his pace had slowed to little more than a crawl. Nickolai finally stopped the old ox and examined his foot. The foot had picked up a rock, so Nickolai removed it.

He stood up and sighed before slapping Maksim on the hindquarters. There was no longer any point in using the ox goad to urge Maksim along. He simply let the ox go at his own pace.

Evening finally came, putting both Nickolai and Maksim out of their misery. They had managed only five loads from the spring. Ten barrels of water—that was a good day's work, but not near enough to move them closer to Nickolai's goal.

Nickolai's confidence was waning. He had thought a Sabbath day's rest would be a sure thing. Didn't God want him to have His Sabbath off? So what had gone wrong? Why hadn't things worked out between him and old Maksim? Why hadn't God helped him get the number of loads he needed to fill his quota by Friday night? Did God have other plans? Did God want him to spend another ten days in the box? Had that been His original plan for Nickolai all along?

Nickolai's brow knit in a furrowed frown. It didn't matter. He knew he wouldn't work on Sabbath even with the ultimatum from the warden hanging over his head.

There just seemed no way out! No way to turn!

CHAPTER 26

By now Nickolai had no idea what God had in store. He was at a total loss as to what he should expect, or what he should do next.

Sixteen barrels of water. There was no way he could haul that many by sunset the next day—ten for Friday, and then the extra six to make up the ten he would need for the Sabbath supply. There just wasn't time.

Nickolai had been doing his part all week, but it didn't seem to him that God was doing His. He had not answered Nickolai's prayers—at least not yet, and certainly not in the way Nickolai would have thought things should go. And from all appearances it looked like the window of opportunity was closing fast.

The whole thing left Nickolai totally discouraged. Would he get to have his Sabbaths off? His faith wanted to say yes, but his logic said no. He had worked late Wednesday, and then well after dark again on Thursday, but with only four extra barrels of water to show for it.

Nickolai spent a long time on his knees in earnest prayer that night, even losing precious sleep to talk to his heavenly Father. He had to find a way to solve his dilemma. He had to succeed, somehow.

Eventually he dropped off into a troubled sleep. Somewhere in the night he awoke, still on his knees in prayer.

As Nickolai climbed onto his bunk, a sudden thought struck him full in the face. Could it be that all his efforts to bring the water to the camp had been done on his own terms? Was it possible that he had been so anxious to earn a Sabbath day's rest that he had begun to rely on his own efforts to get it?

A Bible story came to mind, and Nickolai wondered if his situation might be proving to be somewhat similar.

God had called Gideon to lead the Israelite tribes against a common enemy, the Amalekites. The Israelites had rallied to arms, answering Gideon's call by the thousands. In fact 32,000 of them had come, anxious for battle and ready to serve. Or were they?

Evidently God saw things differently than Gideon did.

Two different tests were given—first, Gideon was told to send soldiers home if they were the least bit afraid, and second, all but 300 men were asked to leave because they weren't really ready for battle.

Gideon was dismayed that God expected so much with so little to work with, and that's exactly how Nickolai was feeling right now. How was he going to keep the Sabbath day holy if he didn't even have time, or the ox, on his side?

Nickolai half-smiled a crooked grin in the darkness. Right now he would be glad if he could have had 300 oxen on his side.

He turned over and tried to go to sleep. Like Gideon, Nickolai was beginning to realize that even if it were possible to bring in enough loads by Friday sunset, the triumph and the credit were not to be his. He had wanted to do things his way, not that his motive and intentions hadn't been pure. It was just that the plans had all been his.

He knew that God wanted him to have Sabbath off. There was no question about that. From the day Nickolai had arrived at the prison camp, he had been honoring the Sabbath. And he had suffered for it, but Nickolai thanked God every day that he had never given in and given up his loyalty to God's holy day.

But the testing time was evidently not over. This time around he wasn't being tested by being cooped up in a prison box. It was a different sort of test—one that required incredible amounts of energy and determination and patience.

But in the end he knew the victory would be God's. God was no doubt working things out for an even greater purpose than Nickolai could imagine. It had to be that! What else could it be?

If Nickolai was being tested like Gideon, then it must be that his own plans would have to give way to God's plans. The way Nickolai had been doing things left little chance for the men in camp to give God credit for anything resembling a miracle. But Nickolai was now beginning to see that if God had things His way, they wouldn't have a choice.

It felt good to surrender everything to God once again. Nickolai had always believed in giving God full control. It was like second nature to him, and he lamented the fact that he had allowed himself to get off track.

Somewhere just before Nickolai dropped off to sleep, his mind drifted once again to one of his favorite Bible verses: "All things work together for good to those who love God, and are called according to His purpose."

CHAPTER 27

Morning came too early for Nickolai. After all the moments of discouragement during the previous two days of work, Nickolai had begun to falter in his faith.

And then he remembered that he had woken in the night to a moment of inspiration, an amazing epiphany that his experience was actually very biblical. Like Gideon, Nickolai once again realized that he was going to have to trust in his heavenly Father. He was going to have to place his faith in the One who could make all things work together for good.

The day and the ultimate challenge had arrived, and Nickolai went out to meet them. He hurried to the barn to rouse old Maksim to the task of the day. But to his surprise Maksim was already on his feet, his legs restless and his eyes fully alert.

"Well, well, this is a change!" Nickolai mused. "You're never on your feet this early in the morning!" He gave the old ox a swat on the rump.

Every day this week when he had come to the stables, he always found Maksim lying down.

But now Maksim was yanking at his chain, ready to go.

Nickolai threw old Maksim's harness over his neck and back and strapped it on. "Alright, old boy!" he announced cheerfully. "Let's get going!"

For a moment Nickolai's heart lifted at the thought of Maksim's high energy level. It was encouraging and even refreshing to see the animal finally in sync with the man. Of course it was a bit late now, Nickolai mused to himself.

But when Nickolai led Maksim out of the shed and hitched him to the cart, the animal lurched forward as though he were on his way to a race. Nickolai would have liked to stop by the kitchen for some cold turnips and Russian bread as he had other mornings this week, but he never had a chance. Old Maksim headed out of camp at a run, and it was all Nickolai could do to keep up with him. In fact, Nickolai ended up running all the way to the spring behind Maksim and the bouncing, bumping cart.

When Maksim finally pulled the cart to a stop, his tongue was hanging out, and his soft beige coat was wet with sweat. Nickolai tried to catch his breath as he stepped up to the ox now also breathing heavily.

"Wow! What was that all about!" was all Nickolai could say as Maksim stood with his head down, his eyes rolling up in his head.

Nickolai filled the water barrels and then pulled a rope from the cart and tied the barrels on securely. In case Maksim got any ideas about running again, Nickolai wanted the barrels to stay on the cart.

He looked at the ox again. What was up with the big animal? The day before the whole operation had nearly come to a grinding halt because Maksim had no energy. Now he had enough energy for ten oxen, and it appeared that he was running to beat all records. It was as though someone had built a fire under him.

Nickolai knew he couldn't afford to stand around wondering about this amazing spectacle that had occurred before his very eyes. He needed to capitalize on the opportunity Maksim was offering—the gift that God had given him.

Nickolai quickly put the wooden lids on the barrels. The old ox had made the trip in such a short time that Nickolai had to wonder, just how fast had it been, exactly?

But he didn't have any time to think about it, because suddenly, as if on cue, the ox started out again. He strained against the harness until the cart was rumbling along at a fairly good pace. The old ox was moving at unheard-of speeds.

But the most bizarre thing about it all was the way Maksim was doing it. His big angular body was gliding along as if in fluid motion. His gait, steady and smooth, pulled the cart along without the lurching motion that usually came because of the play between the harness and the cart shafts.

And then suddenly Nickolai remembered a dream that he had had at the beginning of the week about Maksim and him racing to the spring. It had all been a wonderful fantasy then. Now it was an exciting reality.

Nickolai knew he had never seen anything quite like this. It was remarkable how the old animal had run to the spring on the first trip, but the return trip was even more incredible! No one would believe him if he told them. They would have had to see it to even comprehend it. How could he explain to them the peculiar sight of the ox trotting briskly along with heavy water barrels on a cart on an empty road in the wastelands of Siberia? The whole thing was just uncanny!

And now he and Maksim were making incredible time! The old ox ran and ran and ran! There was no doubt in Nickolai's mind that God was the source of Maksim's boundless energy. It was wonderful to see God demonstrating Himself in this miraculous way. It was truly a marvel and an inspiration to the preacher.

The real question was, why now? Why had God waited until the last day to help Nickolai? Of course Nickolai knew the answer to that question. God wanted to remove all doubt from Nickolai's mind that there was anything he could do himself to work out his own miracle story.

CHAPTER 28

And so the morning flew by. By noon they had already made five trips. Nickolai was speechless. What could he say? God was performing an astonishing miracle and doing it in a way that Nickolai could never have predicted.

All afternoon the two of them hustled. Nickolai grew weary from his continual running after the ox and cart. It was almost ridiculous. All week he had been trying to get the ox to run, but he had failed miserably.

Now he was the one running just to keep up with the ox, and it was wearing him out. After his regular trips to the box, his muscles had truly atrophied, but that was another incredible part about this whole amazing miracle. Nickolai had energy and full use of his legs. True, his leg muscles were no longer tough and sinewy as they had once been, but he was keeping up and his legs weren't failing him. There was something to be said for that!

Although he was growing bone weary and short of breath, he would not allow himself to ride in the cart, even if just out to the spring with empty barrels. He knew he just couldn't take the chance of wearing the ox out. Old Maksim had to be nearing the breaking point! How could he sustain that speed and intensity for all these hours?

Nickolai kept thinking the ox would drop any minute, but he didn't—he just kept going and going and going. It was nothing short of a miracle indeed! Without a shadow of a doubt, nothing short of God's Spirit was keeping the ox on his feet.

It was all so exciting how things had transpired. Nickolai dared not stop for fear they would somehow lose the momentum Maksim had gained. By the time the shadows of late afternoon had turning to evening, they had completed seven trips to the spring. They only needed to make one last trip.

Would they make it by sunset? Was Nickolai pressing his luck at taking Maksim out one more time?

Fortunately, Maksim had his own ideas. When Nickolai turned the cart around and paused to check the angle of the sun in the sky, the ox headed out of camp without hesitation.

Nickolai was famished, but he had no choice. He had to follow. He had managed to grab a loaf of bread when he drove by the kitchen about noon, but that was all he had gotten to eat.

That last trip to the spring was the hardest of all. It seemed to Nickolai that it would never end. By now Maksim had slowed a bit, but the stop at the spring gave him a much-needed rest. He drank long and deep at the spring as he had so many times already that day.

But when Nickolai put the lids on the barrels and turned the cart around, Maksim took off just like every other trip. Again Nickolai had to run to keep up, but they both had their second wind now, and it was as if nothing could deter them. God had truly blessed them with a will and the energy to succeed. The Sabbath rest was looking really good by now.

Never in his life had he looked forward so much to resting on the Lord's holy day! Never had he been so sure that God was working behind the scenes to perform a miracle to end all miracles! And all for the sake of a Russian pastor who had dedicated himself to honor God and His memorial of Creation.

As they raced across the steppes of the Siberian plain, the shadows lengthened even further. Many creatures were stirring for the evening now. The lemmings were gathering by the score on the hummocks of sedge grass, squeaking and chattering their rodent talk. A lone snowy owl again eyed them from his perch of tundra sod. And on the rise to the north, a half dozen Russian prairie wolves were sitting, waiting for the moon to come up. They watched with interest as the man and ox raced by, the cart bumping and jostling along.

Amazingly enough, Nickolai never even gave the wolves a thought. Ordinarily, he might have been afraid of their numbers, and maybe he should have been, but honestly, he really didn't have the time to dilly-dally. He had a Sabbath to prepare for, and the camp was just in sight around the bend. This was not a time to be afraid of a wolf attack. God had performed a miracle for the preacher and the ox, and right now Nickolai was sure a hundred wolves would not have been able to detain them.

Maksim pulled in to camp, his legs still trotting. Only when the cart pulled up to the kitchen did his legs stop churning. Only then did the man allow himself to stop and catch his breath.

There sat the other eight full barrels of water, waiting to be used the next day. The sun hadn't quite yet set, but it was very near to doing so. With God's help, Nickolai had completed the impossible task that he had set out to do.

As he slid the barrels down the skid ramps set against the cart, Nickolai bowed his head and breathed a sigh of relief. The miracle was complete! There was no other explanation for the job they had been able to accomplish! God had truly done His part.

In the far-reaching shadows of the waning day, a well-known verse came to Nickolai's mind. "Not by might, nor by power, but by My Spirit, says the Lord of hosts."

Never in Nickolai's life had a verse of Scripture held such meaning. Never had a text been so rich with significance. Truly Nickolai had triumphed over the test that had threatened to undo his faith, and the victory was sweeter than anything he had experienced or ever imagined.

CHAPTER 29

The last rays of the late-setting, summer sun were cutting across the landscape as Nickolai took Maksim to the stable. He hurriedly unhooked Maksim from the cart and pulled the harness from his neck and shoulders. Then he gave the tired ox some sedge grass and slapped him on the rump.

"I want you to enjoy this rest, Maksim. You deserve it!" He stepped to the stable doorway, and then turned to the old ox one last time. "I hope you know I won't be coming for you tomorrow morning. We don't have to work at all tomorrow. We've earned a rest—both of us—and we're going to get it."

Nickolai went to one of the water barrels, scooped some water out with a wooden bucket, and headed back to the barracks. It was time for a good bath.

When he was dressed in the only other shirt and pair of clothes he owned, he went to the kitchen for something to eat before Petya closed the kitchen for the night. As usual, he was late for supper, but as usual, Petya had a bowl of borsch waiting for him. He also had a side order of Russian black bread and a rare slab of cheese.

"Well, this is a delicacy!" Nickolai smiled as he savored a bite of the yellow cheese. "Where'd you get it? It's got to be the best treat I've seen in camp yet."

"An old man who lives not far from here has a few reindeer he's tamed. He milks some of the does, and then makes cheese. I was surprised," the cook added, cutting off a thin slice of the cheese for himself. "It does taste pretty good for reindeer cheese, but then again I've never eaten reindeer cheese before, so I guess I don't know what it's supposed to taste like."

After supper Nickolai ambled over to the warden's office to give him the news. He had managed to haul the needed water barrels for the Sabbath hours.

The warden looked up from his desk in surprise. "You've got ten barrels in camp right now full of water?"

"Yes, sir." Nickolai tried not to sound too happy. He didn't want the warden to think of some extra task he might need done. That would be a dirty trick, even for the warden, Nickolai thought.

"Very well, then, Panchuk. Go on and rest. You deserve it. I understand you've been putting in some pretty late nights." The warden turned back to what he had been doing.

"Oh, and Panchuk," he added as he stared at Nickolai over the top of his horn-rimmed glasses, "what was with the ox today? They told me the animal was going wild on you. Wouldn't stop running."

Nickolai smiled sheepishly. "Yes, sir, he was a bit overwrought."

"Overwrought!" the warden nearly burst out laughing. "According to everyone who saw him, he was more like—crazy!"

"Yes, sir, I'd have to agree with you there. A bit crazy. I can't account for it, but—he was—well—we'll just say God helped us get the water in."

How could Nickolai explain what he really thought? That God had spooked the old ox? Or put a bug in his ear? Or given him a shot of adrenalin that had lasted all day?

Perhaps he should have told the warden more about the power of his God. Perhaps, but then it didn't matter because the warden didn't really want to know, and was waving him off.

And so the Sabbath began for Nickolai. He didn't flaunt his time off. Instead he stayed inside the barracks and prayed most of the day. The other prisoners all went to their work assignments, so he had the time to himself. Even the guards left him alone.

Over and over again he thanked God for the miracle performed on his behalf. God had indeed done a marvelous thing, and He had done it with a dumb ox. The whole thing reminded Nickolai of the story in the Bible where God had used a donkey to be His mouthpiece.

The donkey hadn't really wanted to be part of the whole adventure. But like Maksim, he had been drawn unwittingly into the grand plot of the story when Balaam decided to disobey God. On the road to Moab, an angel of God tried to prevent Balaam and his donkey from going on a mission to curse Israel. Balaam didn't know that of course, and he gave the donkey the beating of its life. The poor old donkey put up quite a fuss and then started talking.

Nickolai thought about the similarities between Maksim and Balaam's donkey. Like Balaam's donkey, Maksim had been used by God to be His witness. Like the donkey, Maksim was a part of a wonderful miracle that might very well be told down through the years of time.

The day turned out to be a grand day for rest and relaxation for Nickolai, and he enjoyed the fruit of his labors with relish. He couldn't remember when he had felt a more complete peace. And he slept some. He deserved it, he felt, for all the nights of short sleep, and for having to run behind the ox cart all day on Friday. He figured that he had run some 24 or 25 kilometers.

Nickolai went to the mess hall somewhere near sunset. All of the men had already eaten when he arrived, so Petya let him come back into the kitchen and eat there so they could talk.

CHAPTER 30

Is it true?" the cook asked, a gleam of admiration in his eye. Nickolai smiled humbly. "You mean about old Maksim?"

"Exactly. I know you got your quota of barrels, but I also heard that you brought in eight cart loads of water in one day."

Nickolai shrugged his shoulders and kept on smiling.

"That's sixteen barrels of water, preacher man!" Nickolai knew Petya wasn't making fun. The name sounded more like a term of endearment coming from Petya.

"That's right. It's more than I ever managed before."

"Ha!" Petya grunted. "I hear it's a record! More than anyone ever hauled in one day!"

"That so?" Nickolai knew he had to share the whole story with Petya. He couldn't let Petya think that it had been his doing—or even old Maksim's, for that matter. If anyone would understand, Petya would.

"I can't take credit for all that water I hauled yesterday."

Petya stared at him with raised eyebrows.

"That's right. You see, I'm a man of prayer, Petya. After those two years in the box, I learned to depend on God for everything. He helped me deal with the pain and hunger. He gave me peace of mind when I needed it most. And I thank Him especially for life. I owe Him my life, many times over."

"So your God helped you haul all that water? How did He do that?"

"By giving old Maksim super amounts of stamina and energy and inspiration. Strength enough to go all day, running constantly without even stopping to eat. And inspiration to do it in the first place. A little water was all he had and a few carrots I brought along for him."

Petya shook his head. "Well I did find the part about the ox almost unbelievable. Does the warden know all this?"

"I don't think so. I didn't tell him. He didn't ask."

Petya sat on a stool staring at Nickolai. "Did you ask God to do that for you?"

"I didn't ask Him to do that specifically for me because I didn't know it was possible." Nickolai shook his head. "But I did ask my God to please help me find some way to haul enough water so that I wouldn't have to work on the Sabbath."

"So your God came up with this, huh? Pretty neat!" Petya looked pensive. "Does your God help everyone who asks?"

"Everyone who comes to Him in faith. Everyone who seeks Him with all their heart, and soul, and mind."

"And that's what you do?"

"As a Christian pastor, I must say I have always done that. By His grace."

There was silence in the kitchen for quite some time. The only sound that could be heard was the sound of the hot kitchen stove popping and snapping as it slowly cooled for the night.

"Would He do such a thing for me?" Petya asked earnestly, and Nickolai could hardly believe his ears. Here was a man wanting God to come into his life and touch him. This man was asking the essential question of every seeker who had ever come to Jesus—"What must I do to be saved?"

Nickolai went to bed that night, inspired and energized for another week. What the week would bring was anybody's guess, but one thing was for sure, he would have more time this week so he wouldn't have to kill himself, or Maksim. He wouldn't have to run the ox into the ground every day to get the water he would need. This week he would need to bring in seventy barrels of water in six days.

Earlier than usual the next morning, Nickolai was in the barn hitching Maksim up to the cart. But strangely enough Maksim was in no hurry to get going. It was as if all the energy had gone out of his bones, as if he had used up Sunday's energy supply on Friday. Try as he might, Nickolai was powerless to get old Maksim going.

By the end of the day, they had managed to bring in only ten barrels of water, and they had to work after dark to do it.

Monday was no better. It seemed that the harder Nickolai pushed Maksim, the slower he moved. Did the old ox know something Nickolai didn't? Was he playing some kind of silly game just to pit his wits against the man? Was it some kind of a standoff again, where Maksim did what he wanted, when he wanted?

Or was it nothing of the sort? Had the previous Friday just been a freak accident of nature? Had it been an incredible, unexplainable phenomena of animal behavior that no one had ever seen, and would never see again?

Nickolai had hoped that on Tuesday he might make up for the loads he had failed to haul on the first two days of the week. But Tuesday was a bust too, and the outcome worried Nickolai, leaving him feeling frustrated and confused.

He was now getting up so early every morning that he had to wonder if he was losing all touch with reality. What kind of a life was this? He was going to bed at night after everyone else, and then getting up before anyone in camp had even stirred. By dawn he and Maksim were usually already on their way to the spring.

On Wednesday they made some progress. Old Maksim seemed to have new life in his step once again, and he moved with purpose all that morning.

By mid-afternoon it was clear to Nickolai that they would be able to bring in at least seven loads. That was an extra four barrels toward his goal of ten. Nickolai was still holding out hope that there might be a chance of filling his quota by Friday night.

Maksim was moving with a purpose now, and he didn't let up all day. Nickolai felt so good about the rate at which they were working now that he found himself singing an old hymn. "Oh God our help in ages past, our hope for years to come. Our shelter from the stormy blast, and our eternal home. Under the shadow of Thy throne, still may we dwell secure. Sufficient is Thine arm alone, and our defense is sure."

Nickolai could feel the power of the Holy Spirit beside him out there on the lonely road to the spring. He raised his hands to the sky as he sang the final verse of the old hymn in a throaty baritone voice.

"Oh God our help in ages past, our hope for years to come. Be Thou our Guide while life shall last, and our eternal home."

Nickolai went to bed that night feeling that the day had been a success, but he secretly dreaded the coming of another day. What chance did he have of making the quota? If he could somehow haul seven loads the next day, it would be their only hope. Seven loads on Thursday would give them a total of eight barrels toward the extra ten they needed, but he knew they could haul no less. Even so, that would still leave them with another six trips needed on Friday.

Unfortunately, Thursday was a bomb again. Maksim was back to his old tricks of poking along the windswept road to the spring. If the situation hadn't seemed so serious to Nickolai, he might have taken the time to feel sorry for the old ox. Now all he had time for was exasperation.

At the end of the long day they had managed to bring in a measly ten barrels. They had only made five trips, two trips short of his goal. They were now six extra barrels short of the tally they would need to bring in by Friday sunset.

And with that realization, still far short of their goal, all of Nickolai's hopes died.

CHAPTER 31

On Friday morning Nickolai didn't even bother to get out of bed early. What was the point? It wouldn't be possible for them to finish the job by sunset anyway. There were just too many barrels of water to bring into camp by the time the Sabbath would begin.

It didn't seem to matter that Nickolai had prayed and worked hard all week again, stretching every fiber of his being to add to the number of barrels needed. It had all been for nothing.

Finally just after dawn Nickolai got up and headed for the kitchen. There was no sense of urgency now. He could afford to get some breakfast this morning.

On his way to the kitchen, another prisoner called out to him. "You'd better go to the stables and check on that old ox. I think he's gone crazy! He's making a lot of racket in there!"

Nickolai stopped in his tracks. He wanted to ignore the man's announcement, but a faint hope of something a week old flickered in his heart. It wasn't possible was it? Could Maksim be thinking of trying to run a repeat performance?

Nickolai turned and headed for the stables, and the closer he got, the more optimistic he became. Old Maksim was indeed going berserk, if that was really him making all the noise! It sounded as if he was trying to pull the stable down, posts and all!

"I don't believe it!" Nickolai yelled, rushing through the open stable door. There stood Maksim, yanking on his chain and pawing at the ground impatiently.

Nickolai surveyed the scene for only a moment, and then he flew into action. If old Maksim wanted to haul water barrels, then that is what they would do. It was later than Nickolai would have liked it to be, and he wished with all his heart now that he had gotten up by faith and done his part. But he had not, and so he had to make up for the hour or so he had wasted in bed—if God would be so merciful.

SDO-4

It was a strange and almost comical feeling Nickolai had as he hurriedly unhooked Maksim from his chain, threw the harness over his neck and shoulders, and hitched him to the ox cart. All week he had worked early and late to accomplish his purpose. It had been all he could think of day and night.

But then when things didn't turn out as he had planned, his faith had floundered and he had lost sight of the goal. What a shame—Nickolai scolded himself over and over again! Now, when he desperately needed to be up and on his way, he had been sleeping on the job.

"Forgive me, Lord," he fervently prayed. "I'm not worthy of your goodness. Help me to make up for the lost time. Help Maksim to do his part—he's more worthy of your grace than I."

Nickolai heaved a sigh as he checked the rope that held the barrels securely in place. Sometimes dumb animals weren't so dumb. At least they knew how to listen to God's voice. He thought about the story of Balaam and his donkey again and how God had worked though the actions of an animal. When Balaam couldn't see God's will, a willing donkey had.

And now it appeared God was ready to use Maksim again. The ox was willing—it was the man who lacked the faith.

In short order they were off to the spring. If anyone had been watching, they would have seen the ox running full tilt out of camp, his tail flying and the cart bouncing along behind him, and the man running for all he was worth to keep up. It was as if the ox were on a mission, and indeed he was. No longer did it appear as if the man was in charge. Clearly the ox was in control and determining the pace at which they would work.

On and on he ran as if in a frenzy, as if he had somehow lost his mind. Again Nickolai felt it was the strangest thing he had ever seen. It was as if the angels had built a fire under old Maksim and ignited his spirit to fulfill God's will and greatest wish—that Nickolai be rewarded for his desire to honor God's holy Sabbath. All week it had been Nickolai who had been pushing them hard to bring extra barrels of water to the kitchen, always mindful that they needed a tally of 70 in order to make the mark. And all week Maksim had done his part, but more often than not he had worked with less energy than Nickolai wished he would.

Now it was Friday again, the preparation day, and Maksim was on a mission. The trip to the spring for that first load of water was run in record time. It was not a complete surprise that Maksim was running helter-skelter to and from the spring. Nickolai had witnessed him acting this way the previous Friday, but it was a shock that he was doing it for the second week in a row. It helped to remove any doubt in Nickolai's mind that such a thing might have been a freak accident the week before. As Nickolai ran panting behind the cart all the way back to camp, he had to admit that God works in mysterious ways.

As everyone in camp watched Nickolai and Maksim, it confirmed in their minds, even more than the week before, that the God of heaven was again working on Nickolai's behalf. How else could it be interpreted?

Since entering the camp, Nickolai had been a living testimony of determination and loyalty. The colors of his character were beginning to become obvious to everyone, prisoners and guards, alike. Even the warden had been forced to admit that here was a man of the highest caliber, one who would rather suffer persecution and pain than dishonor the God he served.

And now again, they were witnessing a miracle in action, evidence of the power God was willing to demonstrate on Nickolai's behalf. It was a strange and unusual sight, man and ox running full speed into camp, the ox cart rolling along with two full barrels of water on board. And it was equally bizarre to see Maksim turn the ox cart around and head back to the spring as soon as the full water barrels were taken off and the empty ones dropped into place.

And then the whole performance would repeat itself again as man and beast were seen speeding out of camp and across the wide open spaces of the Siberian steppes.

CHAPTER 32

All that morning Nickolai and Maksim worked, sweat pouring from their bodies. It was an amazing and almost comical sight! As the two could be seen approaching the camp, someone would always signal their arrival with a shout, "Here they come again!"

And then everyone within range would stop whatever it was they were doing—prisoners and guards, alike. Petya would always come out of the kitchen for a look. It was a great way to take a break. By the time Nickolai and Maksim returned to the camp the third time, everyone was cheering and throwing their caps into the air.

Nickolai hardly had time to notice their shouts of encouragement. He did give a tired salute on his entry into camp, and then another wave of his arm again as the cart spun around to make its next trip to the spring.

If Nickolai had been watching on the fourth trip back to camp, he would have noticed that even the warden had stopped what he was doing to come out and see the amazing spectacle.

By noon, they were already heading out for their fifth trip to the spring. As Nickolai hurried to catch up with the ox, Petya ran alongside him and handed him a small bag with cold turnips and Russian black bread in it. Nickolai had managed to drink a little water each time they stopped at the spring and the camp, but he had not thought of eating. Now he realized that he was famished, and he was so grateful for the friendship of this man who was watching out for him.

He ate the turnips as he ran, praying that God would help the food to digest in spite of the conditions in which he was eating the meal.

On the return trip Nickolai saw four or five of the prairie wolves come out and sit in a row to watch the man and ox race by. He tossed a chunk of the black bread to the wolves and watched them fight over it as the cart raced away to the east.

The kilometers became easier to run, and his breathing less strenuous.

It was as if God was giving Nickolai a second and third wind, so he could become part of the miracle in action.

The day melted away as trip after trip was made, until there was only one last run to be made. By now, the man and beast were running in tandem as though this adventure had turned them into a well-oiled machine.

And they finished the task with time to spare. By the time the sun dipped below the western horizon, Nickolai had unloaded the last barrel of water, gone to the barracks to clean up, and was on his way to the kitchen to eat the evening meal he knew Petya would have waiting for him there.

What a day it had been, and what a lesson in faith for Nickolai. In his heart he knew that he would never again doubt God's amazing watch care and His ability to come to the aid of a soul in need. Of course, Nickolai believed in the power of God to protect and preserve, and He knew of God's willingness to act on behalf of his children in time of need. But he had never experienced such a dramatic display of God's power to vindicate one of His children. And to everyone in camp this had been a clear demonstration of the lengths to which Nickolai's God would go to honor the pastor for his faithfulness.

As Nickolai sat in the kitchen eating a hot bowl of borsch and sipping a cup of tea, the cook spoke of the electricity that had ignited the camp.

"You did it again!" Petya exclaimed. "It was amazing!"

"We did it!" Nickolai countered. "Maksim and I did it, and we owe it to God from whom all blessings flow."

Petya shook his head in disbelief. "I wish you could have seen the two of you!" he crowed. "What a sight!" He handed Nickolai another slice of black bread. "You two are like celebrities here in camp now. I don't suppose the warden will ever give you trouble again. He can't. The guards won't let him!"

On his way back to the barracks, Nickolai stopped to watch the moon rising in the east. The orange oval of light looked warm and inviting, like the feeling he had in his chest. For the first time since arriving in camp over two years ago, he felt exhilaratingly free.

And God was responsible for it. It had taken a while for Nickolai to see his prayers fully realized, but in the end things had worked out for the best with God being justified and Nickolai feeling vindicated. Nickolai decided that it was always best to fully trust in God's timing, because only God could see the end from the beginning.

As Nickolai turned to enter the barracks, he could hear the prairie wolves howling somewhere in the distant darkness, but the sound no longer made him feel lonely. He remembered feeling lost and forlorn when he had first arrived in camp. The sound of the prairie wolves had left him feeling empty, and he had even been tempted to feel abandoned by God. But not any longer.

Clearer than ever before was his faith in Jesus. It was a moment of truth for him, and it thrilled him through and through to know that God was with him even on the wastelands of the Siberian tundra. To have a peace like that was truly worth dying for, but of course it didn't look as if that was what God required now. He had stood the test and he had come through shining.

CHAPTER 33

Nickolai reaped the benefits of the second Friday miracle even more than he had the first. Again he spent time in prayer, thanking God for His wonderful gift of rest on the holy Sabbath day. Again he had a chance to escape his labors of the week.

All that following week Nickolai and Maksim worked together to bring the needed water to the camp. And all that week, strangely enough, Maksim worked at a normal pace.

It was amazing! The slow pace at which Maksim persisted in working Sundays through Thursdays was almost as phenomenal as his working to beat the band on Friday. But by Friday sunset, the extra ten barrels of water for the Sabbath were again ready and waiting at the kitchen. The whole thing was a spectacular miracle to Nickolai.

As the weeks passed, Nickolai and Maksim settled into their routine. Sundays through Thursdays always brought just a little bit of consternation to Nickolai. Why did Maksim have to poke along all week, and then run lickety-split on Fridays? What was he trying to prove? Didn't he ever learn? Or was that it at all? Was Maksim just operating, in fact, on the instinctive impressions the Holy Spirit was giving him?

But there was another thing. Nickolai always felt funny knowing that on Friday the ox would be performing his marathon run. It made him feel presumptuous and just a little bit guilty knowing that he could relax and just let God make the Friday miracle happen.

But it was out of Nickolai's hands, and apparently that's the way God wanted it. In the final scope of things, Nickolai's worries had ended up being fairly redundant anyway. What was most important now was the fact that the man and ox were proving to be a real witness at the prison camp.

The weather turned cooler in August with more rain falling than Nickolai remembered from previous years. Many days he had to work in the rain, and he suffered from the dampness of it all. Some days the rain turned to sleet and ice, and on the days it didn't rain, frost fell thick and hard. Petya loaned him a raincoat, for which Nickolai was grateful. What would he have done without such a friend?

After work many evenings, Nickolai spent time talking to Petya. Sometimes they talked in the kitchen, sometimes in the barracks. Sometimes they talked late into the night. But they talked less and less of prison life, and more and more on eternal things.

One evening in the kitchen, Petya came right to the point. "You've been such an inspiration to me since you came to this camp. You've suffered so much for God, and yet you are still faithful to Him. I'm so inspired by the hope you've brought us all." Petya stared at the floor solemnly. "Can you help me find this peace you carry with you everywhere you go? I want the power of this peace in my life too."

Nickolai laid his hand on Petya's shoulder. "Believe in the Lord Jesus Christ," he said. "If you do this you'll have God's peace when you need it most."

"You've said that before," Petya raised his eyes to stare at Nickolai unbelievingly. "Can it be true that it's really that simple?"

"God has made it simple, Petya. He's not willing that anyone should perish. Trust me on this one. It's the one thing that has always given me courage to live for Him every day." Nickolai rubbed his tired eyes.

Petya blew out the kerosene lamp, and then closed the door to the kitchen. As the two men stepped out into the night, the moon was full, rising quickly from the horizon. Not a sound could be heard except the mournful call of a snowy owl somewhere in the night.

"I want to be baptized." Petya suddenly announced. His voice was soft, but there was a note of determination in it. "I believe in everything you've told me because I've seen the power of God in your life."

Nickolai looked at Petya in surprise. This man had gleaned more from their conversations than he would have guessed!

There was silence for several moments as Nickolai caught his breath. "Praise God!" he finally said, and then bowed his head in reverence. Petya was giving his heart to Jesus! The very thought of it made Nickolai's heart race. Was this to be his first convert in Siberia? After three long years in this prison camp, was the fruit of his labor going to finally pay off?

"Would there be some way you could baptize me?" Petya continued.

"Yes—yes of course!" Nickolai quickly replied, but it was more of an attempt to assure himself than Petya.

"Where will we find enough water?"

"Well, there's the water we bring to camp," Nickolai thought for a moment, "but the barrels aren't big enough to submerge you in."

"What about the spring? Is there enough water there?"

"Yes, of course, but the water isn't deep. I'd have to dig it deeper."

"Can you do it, Pastor?"

Nickolai put his hand on Petya's shoulder and smiled. It was the first time Petya had referred to him personally as pastor. "We'll get it done, Petya. I will dig the spring deeper. Maybe a little bit every time I go out to the spring for the barrels of water. We'll find a way."

CHAPTER 34

It took some work, but Nickolai was able to do as they had planned. Digging a water hole at the spring was quite easy. Planning when they would go through with the baptism was a bit trickier.

On a Friday night after the men in camp had all gone to sleep, Nickolai and Petya snuck out behind the barracks and circled around to the opposite side of camp. Once on the road they began the long walk to the spring. It was a risk—no doubt prairie wolves were watching their every move. But the baptism went off without a hitch. Fortunately for them, the evening was warmer than most that time of year. Both men stood in the water hole at the spring, savoring the joy of the sacred experience. Afterwards they walked the distance to camp, singing a hymn Nickolai had taught Petya and shivering in the dampness of the cool evening.

And then summer was gone, and fall seemed to pass them by completely. Before they knew it, snow flurries began to fall, the reindeer started to migrate, and snow geese flew southward through the skies.

By October, winter had settled in. Nickolai was glad for the long underwear the warden supplied him with. In spite of their past, he began to feel a warm spot in his heart now for the warden. To Nickolai it seemed the warden was trying to say in some simple way that he was sorry for all the trouble he had given him.

The days were short, but that didn't change the number of barrels needed each week. I order to bring in the required quota, Nickolai and Maksim found themselves working in the dark several hours before dawn each morning, and then three or four hours again after sunset.

The ice was forming thick at the spring now, and Nickolai had to use an ax to cut through it. Of course, this took time and made the trips longer, but Nickolai had other things to worry about.

In the cold, dark hours of the winter, Nickolai knew he needed to be watchful of the wolves. Food was scarce now on the tundra, so a man and an ox might prove tempting to their hungry stomachs.

But God was merciful, and although Nickolai and Maksim had a few scares, they managed to stay alive and well.

The cold, hard winter passed somehow, and then spring gave way to summer. By now Nickolai had accepted the fact that he might be in this prison camp for a very long time. When he was tempted to wonder why God needed him in this remote tundra outpost, he remembered Petya's decision for Jesus.

And he contemplated the salvation of the other 300 men who were imprisoned at the camp. More than anything he wanted them to know God as he did. Eventually he started Bible studies with those who were interested, and before long there was a small band that met regularly.

For seven more years Nickolai spent his days at the remote prison camp on the steppes of Siberia. For seven years he worked with Maksim to haul water from the spring. For all those years he remained a constant witness to the power of God in the life of a dedicated Christian.

To the men in camp, the life and work of Nickolai and Maksim became a living testimony. Visitors who came to camp witnessed the phenomenon themselves. Those who left the prison told of a man and ox that ran all day every Friday, so they could rest all day Saturday.

And then one day the army officer who had freed Nickolai from the crate came back to the prison camp. When he saw Nickolai and Maksim hauling water, he remembered the incident from eight years before.

But now he was told quite a different story. When he heard about Maksim's strange habit of running all day Friday to bring two day's supply of water in one, he was amazed.

With great interest he asked Nickolai about the operation, and Nickolai shared the whole incredible tale. He told how desperate he had been those first few weeks trying to get Maksim to haul enough water fast enough to earn a Sabbath day's rest. And of course he told how good God had been to him. He explained how the ordeal had tested his faith in God, and how he had almost given up.

The miracle of Maksim's marathon run that first Friday stirred the colonel's heart, and the repeat performance the following Friday was even more surprising to him. The colonel could see that Nickolai was a good man. He could see clearly now that the preacher had not been guilty of insubordination. In fact, the testimony of his daily life was proof that he had been willing all along to do whatever was asked of him. Most importantly, the colonel saw that Nickolai had been faithful to his God. Without a doubt he had been willing to do whatever his God had asked of him.

The colonel then shocked Nickolai by taking him to the warden's office to announce that he was going to sign his release forms. He was free to go home on the train to be with his family once again.

"You have shown us all what a man of character can do if he is motivated," the colonel said proudly. "And you have shown what devotion can do for a man who loves his God."

The colonel chuckled, and then added, "I guess none of us have ever seen an animal as crazy as your ox. If you and your God can get a stubborn ox to run like that, you could probably do just about anything!"

With tears in his eyes, Nickolai thanked the colonel for his kindness. And then he took his few personal belongings, followed the colonel and his horse back to the train, and began the long journey back to Kiev.

Nickolai returned to the life of a pastor and continued to witness for God during the good times as he had during the bad. His church members rejoiced with him that God had brought him home from his long ordeal, and they thanked Jesus for his faithfulness under fire.

Today, like every other Seventh-day Adventist Christian in the former Soviet Union, Nickolai Panchuk waits for Jesus to come again. One day soon he will see Jesus coming in the clouds of heaven and hear the words, "Well done my good and faithful servant. You have been faithful to me in small things and in big. You have suffered for my sake. Come and enter into the joy of your Lord."

CHAPTER 35

But that's not the end of the story. After Nickolai left for home, a new prisoner came to camp who knew nothing of the man and ox who ran all day on Fridays so they could rest on Saturdays.

The new man, Gennadi, was also given the job of hauling water from the spring every day, and he quickly learned to plod along behind the ox cart. Like Nickolai he knew that the job was the one most hated by all the men in camp. No one else wanted to do all that walking.

However, he also discovered that Maksim was stubborn and would refuse to do anything that was not part of his regular regiment. The old ox refused to be hurried. He refused to be intimidated. He refused to continue working after dark.

Not surprisingly, Gennadi soon came to admit that he wasn't the one in charge while on their trips to the spring. Maksim obviously was. They were up at the crack of dawn every day, plodding laboriously back and forth to the spring, but always on Maksim's own terms.

But on that first Friday morning, Gennadi was in for the surprise of his life. The old ox fairly ran his legs off all day, and Gennadi was so shocked he didn't know what to think.

No one had bothered beforehand to tell him about Maksim's strange habits, or his famous track record. Maybe it was because they wanted to see the look on Gennadi's face when he finally witnessed it for himself. Maybe they were looking forward to hearing the new driver rant on and on about how crazy the old ox was. Maybe it was just that the whole thing had been going on for so long now that they never thought about it as a strange and unusual event anymore.

But on that first Friday morning as Maksim came running back into camp, Gennadi came huffing and puffing along behind him. The poor prisoner looked as though he had been running a race. When he finally came to a stop, he bent over with his hands on his knees, wheezing and desperately trying to catch his breath. Perspiration dripped from his face, and his clothes were completely soaked with sweat.

But if he thought he was going to get a rest, he was in for a second surprise. Maksim never really gave Gennadi time to get his breathing back to normal. No sooner were the water barrels unloaded from the cart, than the old ox took off again in a cloud of dust.

And that was the last anyone saw of them until over an hour later when they came racing back down the road into camp again. This time Gennadi was even further behind.

Who would have thought that an ox pulling a cart full of water barrels would outdo a man running on foot? Of course, Maksim was used to this—he had been doing it for more than eight years now.

The two of them went at it all morning. On the ride out to the spring Gennadi jumped on the cart for a rest. However, when the cart had two full barrels on it, he had to run on foot all the way back. Each time they came racing back into camp, Gennadi would take a few moments to rest, but he knew he dared not wait too long for fear the ox would take off for the spring again with the full water barrels still on the cart.

By late afternoon Gennadi looked as though he had been running a marathon, and it appeared he would drop from exhaustion any moment. He might never have made it through the afternoon had Petya not come to his aid the last few trips to help him unload the full water barrels from the cart.

"What's wrong with that animal!" Gennadi would shout every time he came stumbling into camp. "He's going to kill me!"

Of course everyone just laughed, because they knew the rest of the story and were having their fun at Gennadi's expense.

But by the end of the day, Gennadi could take it no longer. As the sun neared its resting place below the horizon, and old Maksim had pulled the bumping cart into camp for the last time, Gennadi slumped to the ground, his back against the wheel of the ox cart.

"I give up!" he panted and closed his eyes as Petya and several other men gathered around. "The ox is possessed!" he rasped, putting his hands to his head. "There's no other explanation!"

"Yes there is," a voice sounded nearby, and Gennadi turned to see the warden standing behind them.

The warden paused for effect. "You see, that preacher from Kiev has been training old Maksim for years. Nickolai Panchuk refused to work on the seventh day of every week, and he's spoiled the ox with that business of his. Ruined him, and he'll never be the same!"

The warden looked around the circle of men and then directly at Gennadi. "There's no doubt about it in my mind. That preacher made a Sabbath keeper of the ox."

And truly he had. Old Maksim had turned into a seventh-day ox. But it hadn't really been any of Nickolai's doing. The preacher had run side by side with Maksim all those years to bring enough water to last through the Sabbath. And it had always taken a marathon Friday to finish the job each week.

The credit for such a phenomenon was all God's, of course, and everyone who wanted to know the truth had been told so by Nickolai.

Even after Nickolai had left the prison camp and returned home to his family, the influence of his holy life lived on through the testimony of an ox. Old Maksim continued to be true to his duties, ready to be used by his Creator as a witness for the Sabbath.

Nickolai Panchuk was gone, but when there was no one left to share the gospel story, there was still Maksim, the seventh-day ox.

BIBLES
FOR
BREAKFAST

CHAPTER 1

The snow squeaked and crunched under Alexander's feet as he trudged homeward from the train station. It had been a long day, and he was tired. Lately, all the days seemed long for Alexander. He was always tired it seemed.

He stared up at the steel-gray sky growing dimmer by the minute with the coming of dusk. Low banks of clouds pressed down upon the city of Novosibirsk, Russia, making him even more depressed. Would spring never come? Would the damp coldness of winter never end? The trees lining the sidewalk along the street stood mute and naked in the final stages of winter. Stripped of any dignity that was once there's, they waited dormant in their long winter vigil.

Right now that's the way Alexander felt—dormant and listless with no hope of better times to come. A full head of hair and square shoulders made him appear young and strong, but the deep set eyes and dark lines on his face gave him a despondent look.

Alexander was a security officer in a local bank. In many cities, in many countries of the world, the job could have given him a sense of importance, but not in Novosibirsk. Not even the handgun he wore strapped to his thigh in a leather holster could do that. Alexander knew he hadn't gotten the job because he possessed special skills, and he hadn't gotten the job because he knew someone important. He would rather have earned the job based on his qualifications, but as it was, it was just a basic job in security—he was six feet tall and weighed 200 pounds, so he qualified. That's the way jobs were handed out in Novosibirsk. He was no more special than anyone else in the USSR.

Communist Russia had a slogan that was known by everyone and quoted by the masses of the working class: "A job for everyone, and everyone for a job." The expression was intended to bring a sense of security and equality, but somehow for Alexander it didn't ring true today.

He knew he should be content and even grateful for his job. His wife Natasha had a good steady job too as manager of the high-rise apartment complex where they lived. Two incomes were better than one, but even together, their salaries were never enough.

No matter how they managed their money, it was hard to get ahead financially. No matter how much he and Natasha scraped and saved, they just couldn't make their rubles stretch to the end of the month. He would have liked to get a second job, but it wasn't allowed. They didn't own a car, of course. Almost no one did. On top of that, the furniture in their simple flat was drab and unattractive.

And sometimes even food was hard to get, too. Simple things like bread or apples or salt, for instance. Beets, cabbage, and onions were fairly plentiful, but if there were other specialty items people wanted, they had to be patient. Alexander could remember countless times when he had had to stand in line for hours just to get a few rolls of toilet paper. It didn't seem right for a nation that claimed to be the greatest on earth.

He might have been content to live without luxuries, but even the little things in life seemed out of reach. It had been years since Alexander had been able to give his wife something special to wear. It nearly broke his heart every time he saw her looking longingly at a pretty dress in one of the rare foreign magazines that found its way into Novosibirsk. The government did its best to control such propaganda, but from time to time, even newspapers printed pictures of people with status. The women would be dressed splendidly with fashionable hats or furs or nice boots, and always it was the wives of government officials or rich oil tycoons or maybe some KGB officer.

It was at times like this that Alexander felt the worst. If equality was so important in the communist culture, why should some folks have nice things, and others not?

As Alexander slowed his pace, a lone crow landed nearby in the branches of a tree. It cocked its head to one side and cawed raucously, as if to taunt Alexander for his misfortunes in life. Fortunately Alexander had reached home, and he quickly turned up the sidewalk that led to the high-rise apartment complex.

Alexander stepped into the dimly-lit elevator and rode it to their fifth-floor apartment. When he turned the key in the lock, he was met at the door by the family's two dogs, Boris and Lexi, who came running to meet him excitedly.

Like many Russians, Alexander and Natasha loved dogs, and their two Siberian Huskies were the pride and joy of their life. They had no children yet, and this made the bond of affection that much stronger between them and the dogs.

"Boris! Did you miss me?" Alexander grabbed the younger of the two dogs and gave him a bear hug as the overgrown puppy jumped into his arms. The more sedate Lexi approached her master with dignity and poise. Boris was her puppy, but she knew she held the most important place in her master's heart.

The usual greeting by his dogs cheered Alexander after the cold snowy walk home from the train station. For a moment he forgot his troubles as he soaked up the affection. *A dog is truly a man's best friend,* he mused as they licked his hands and clambered for attention. Their thick coats of fur felt warm and soft to his touch, and he knew that they were indeed a blessing to him and Natasha.

Alexander pulled a small paper bag from his pocket and took out a piece of Russian black bread. "Well, Boris, I have one slice of bread from my lunch today. Would you like some of it?" He roughed up the dog's fur, and then broke off a piece to give to Boris, his cavernous mouth a bottomless pit. While Boris gulped the bread, Alexander slipped the remaining piece to Lexi.

"Shall we go for a walk tonight after supper?" he asked the dogs excitedly. Alexander didn't really feel up to walking tonight, but he knew the dogs always waited expectantly for their usual romp in the snow. And they needed the exercise after being cooped up in the small apartment all day.

Unfortunately, they couldn't run free outside while he and Natasha were working. For one thing, it was illegal, and for another, these dogs were handsome animals. They were worth some money, and the envy of everyone who saw them with Alexander when he took them out for a walk.

After the usual welcome, Alexander had time to greet Natasha, his pretty little wife. He gave her a kiss, briefly looking into her blue eyes, and then sat down heavily at the kitchen table. Her soft oval face wreathed in blond curls gazed at him appreciatively as she continued preparing the borsch for their supper. When she noticed his despondent look, she came to stand by his side.

"What is it, Alex?" she asked gently.

"Oh, I'm just feeling sorry for myself," he confessed. "I've had a headache all afternoon. And of course my replacement at the bank came late as usual, so I had to stay longer again. That guy thinks he can come late just because his uncle is a personal friend of the bank manager."

Alexander frowned. "And then the long walk home was cold. The north wind is terrible! These winters just never seem to let up, and this year seems worse than most. I can't imagine what it would be like to live where it is warm all the time." Alexander stopped short in his list of complaints. "I don't know why the cold gets me down like this. Maybe it's a sign of old age."

"Old age? Come now! You're still a young man. Look, you hardly have any gray hairs." Natasha smiled at Alexander and ran her fingers through his thick head of black hair. "When you have white hair on your head or maybe no hair at all, then I'll feel sorry for you."

They laughed together as Natasha continued preparing supper, moving from the stove to the table, from the table to the counter, and then back to the stove again. In his heart Alexander knew that Natasha was the finest woman in all of Novosibirsk. She had to be. She was beautiful and kind and sweet, and to him these made the best combination for a wife.

CHAPTER 2

Alexander and Natasha ate in silence, enjoying one another's company after a long day. The savory borsch smelled so good with its steaming beets, potatoes, cabbage, and garlic. To Alexander it was the best thing for his spirits and his stomach on a night like this. When he had finally eaten his fill of borsch and Russian bread, he pushed his bowl away and leaned back in his chair.

"Something is bothering you tonight," Natasha ventured, "and I don't think it is just the weather."

"You are a wise one, Tash." Alexander half-smiled at her and looked down at his plate. When she didn't get up to clear the table, he finally looked into her face and nodded. "And you're right. Something is bothering me, but I don't think it can be fixed. I'm discouraged." He sighed and shook his head slowly. "The economy is not good now, and prices have been going up everywhere. I need a raise, and so do you. It's been three years since you got that raise of two rubles per month. It's just not enough anymore."

She laid her hand on his, but said nothing.

"Sometimes I feel as though life is so pointless!" he blurted. "I mean, what's the purpose of it all? Why are we here? What do we have to look forward to? Surely there must be something more to life than just getting up in the morning, eating, going to work, coming home, eating again, and going to sleep. There has to be something more! There has to be a reason for life, a meaning for our existence!"

"Think about it!" he kept on. "Babies are born—they grow up, then they marry and have babies of their own. If they're lucky, they grow old and see their grandchildren. And then they die." He shook his head again. "But that's just it, Tasha. There has got to be more to living than just the regular routine of life that comes and goes every day!"

It made Natasha sad to see Alexander like this. Alexander was not a complainer. It wasn't in his nature. He was a good man, a hard worker, and he was not inclined to envy what others had. He was generally a happy man, and the stable one in their marriage. He was always saying the right thing at the right time to assure Natasha of his love and remind her of the future they would have together.

When Natasha's father had died unexpectedly, it was Alexander who made all the arrangements. Natasha's sisters and mother were too shaken up to tend to the details, and even her brother wasn't much use in making the necessary funeral preparations.

But today things were different, and Natasha had to admit that she sensed something had been troubling him lately. He seemed to be slipping into a state of depression that he could not shake. It was as if he were struggling with something unseen, something that lurked beneath the surface of their simple existence, as he put it.

And that was just it. Because it wasn't ordinary, it seemed that Alexander couldn't fix it. Alexander was a proud and strong man, but tonight she knew she needed to just listen and let him talk it out. Maybe that would help.

A sudden knock at the door interrupted their thoughts. The two of them looked at one another. Who could it be? By the sound of the knock it was no doubt a stranger, and at this time of night, that could be a problem.

Alexander got up from the table to answer the door. Was it a neighbor? The police? Even more serious, was it the KGB? Alexander hesitated at the door as he remembered the stories some of his neighbors had told him. When the KGB came calling, they always had reasons. And sometimes, even if a man and his family were innocent, they still paid the price.

That was the name of the game with the KGB—fear and intimidation. The secret police sometimes got out of hand, but who could stop them? Most people were too scared to challenge the system. Once in a while the KGB got themselves in trouble politically, and then they had to bluff their way out of the fixes they got themselves into. But mostly the KGB lived above the law and did what they pleased.

Alexander turned the lock on the door, pulled the bolt aside, and opened the door a crack. To his relief it wasn't the KGB, or even the police. It was a stranger all dressed up in a white shirt, tie, and dress coat.

"Hello!" the handsome young stranger greeted Alexander. "My name is Leonid Serkovsky. I'm a book salesman bringing good news to homes in this neighborhood."

"Good news?" Alexander scoffed, opening the door wider. By now he had gotten over the initial relief of not having to deal with the secret police. "What could possibly be good news?" he argued. "Winter won't end, the price of bread is up, and the local apartment superintendent has refused me the permits I asked for months ago to make improvements on my apartment." Alexander squinted at the book salesman. "And on top of all that, I've had a headache since noon today!"

"I can see that your day has not been good." Leonid shook his head. "Stress is not a good thing. Fortunately, the books I have can help bring new meaning and peace to your life."

"We don't have time for anything that costs money!"

"Do you read, comrade?" Leonid was persistent.

"We're not interested." Alexander reached to close the door, but suddenly Boris and Lexi pushed their way past him through the open doorway and began to sniff the stranger up and down.

"Get back, Boris! Come, Lexi!" Alexander tried to pull the dogs away from Leonid, but the dogs pulled free from his grasp and kept brushing up against Leonid for attention.

"Nice dogs you have here," Leonid offered. "I used to have a Siberian husky when I was young. Gosha was his name—best friend I ever had." He began stroking Lexi's fur. "Your dogs remind me of him so much."

Alexander was intrigued at the ease with which the stranger handled his dogs, and he began to relax. He smiled in spite of his impatience. "Yes, I can certainly see that they like you. I've never seen them so friendly with a stranger."

"Thank you," Leonid's eyes lit up. "I just need a few minutes of your time, sir. As I mentioned before, I have books here in my bag that will bring hope and a new meaning to your life. Good books that can be read over and over again during the long winter months."

"Hmmm. What book cannot be read again and again? That is what books are for. No?

"This is true." Leonid grinned at Alexander's humor. "But these books can do much more." He pulled a Bible from his bag.

"This book here has all the answers to life's questions about good and evil in the world. And this other book is about the history of the Christian Church from Roman times right down to our day." Leonid held up the second book. "It's called *The Great Controversy.*"

CHAPTER 3

Alexander didn't want to admit it, but he was suddenly very interested in what the book salesman was saying. He loved history and read any history book he could get his hands on. In school, history had been his favorite subject—especially ancient history. When he sat down with such a book in the evening, it was hard to put it down. Natasha sometimes had to remind him that it was late and he needed to save some of the book for the next evening.

"You should have been a history professor," she would always laugh.

The salesman was still talking, but Alexander had not yet invited him in.

Suddenly Natasha was at the door. "Alexander! How can you be so rude? Where are your manners?" she scolded. "Don't leave him standing in the doorway! This is a nice man, and I can see that you definitely are interested in what he has brought with him!"

"I'm sorry," Alexander apologized. "Yes, please come in! We don't have much money, but I'm interested in what your books have to say."

Natasha brought Leonid some tea as he began to talk about the two books. "If you have ever wondered about the meaning of life, these books will help," Leonid began.

Alexander stared at Natasha in surprise. *Hadn't they been talking about this very thing just a few minutes earlier?*

"On days when you feel like everything is going wrong, these books can do wonders." Leonid handed Alexander the Bible. "This book will answer many of the questions you have about how to have a healthy life, and how to live longer. It will help you not to worry about whether there will be enough bread for your table, or about whether Russia will be going to war. It will help you have peace in your hearts and know what the future holds."

Leonid's voice grew soft. "Best of all, it will introduce you and your wife to the God of heaven who loves you more than you can imagine, and cares about what happens to you in your life."

"These book will tell us all this?"

"All this and much more," Leonid assured him.

"This is too much to ask of one book." Alexander turned the first few pages of the Bible. "The... Holy... Bible," he slowly read the words. "I've heard of this before. It's a good book."

"The best in the world. I have sold more copies of this than any other."

"Tell me more."

Leonid settled himself in his chair and watched the young couple eagerly looking the book over. It was obvious to him that the Holy Spirit was in this home working on their hearts already. "The Holy Bible is a book inspired by God Himself. It tells of God's plan to make a new world where there will be no more pain and suffering."

"And it will help us to live a better life now?"

"Yes, this is guaranteed."

"Hmmm. What about this other book here? The Great Controversy. It sounds like a book about fighting, and war maybe?"

"In a way it is. It talks about the war between good and evil, between God and Satan. But we don't need to worry. God will win the war and soon come back to take us to live with Him forever in heaven."

Natasha's face brightened, and she leaned forward to get a closer look.

"Your book speaks of this?"

"It does."

She shook her head in amazement. "This book is very good, then."

"The best."

Alexander studied the two books a few moments longer. "Then we will take both of them," he said abruptly.

"A Bible and *The Great Controversy?*"

"Yes. If the message they bring has given us hope already and we haven't even opened them up, think about how our lives will be changed when we read them."

Leonid listened in awe at the testimony these two wonderful people were giving him! Here they were already receptive to the Holy Spirit and the powerful message God had in store for them!

"Do you have copies here tonight that we can buy right now?" Natasha asked excitedly.

"Well, actually no," Leonid admitted. "But I can come back in a few days with a copy for you. Many others have asked for copies this week too, so I must go to my house and get those copies. I could bring them to you in a few days. You may choose which night."

"Should we give you the money right now?"

"You may do that, or you can wait and give me the money when I come again."

Alexander looked at Natasha. "I think we must give him the money now. If he doesn't have enough books for everyone, he will have to give the books to those who have already paid for them, and then we'll have to wait even longer." He looked at Leonid expectantly. "I am right?"

"That is usually the way it works," Leonid replied. He raised a silent prayer of praise to heaven. This was truly an amazing couple. They were so hungry for the Word of God, and already so full of faith that they were willing to pay up front and trust Leonid to bring the books to them.

"Good, then it is settled, but you must stay a while longer and tell us more of what is in these books."

Alexander went to the bedroom to get the rubles needed to pay for the books, while Natasha refilled their cups with hot tea. And Boris and Lexi came to Leonid for more attention and a good scratching behind their ears.

All heaven drew near at the scene before them. Just minutes before, this young couple had been weighed down with the troubles and cares of the world. Now they could feel the power of God working in their home, and already they had a fresh new outlook on life.

CHAPTER 4

Alexander and Natasha had never heard such things before—what Leonid was telling them was truly amazing. It was as if their minds were sponges soaking up all the good things that he was sharing with them about God's plan of salvation for the world. But more importantly, it was touching their hearts personally, making them see everything in their lives from a new perspective.

The couple sat side by side on the couch listening to this young man as he spoke from his heart. Leonid told about the creation of the world and the fall of man, and about God's chosen people down through the ages. And all the things he talked about seemed to make sense, even if it was something they had never heard before.

Creation and evolution were classic examples. Neither Alexander nor Natasha were Christians, so of course they had been taught only the theories of evolution in the Russian schools. They had never heard an alternative explanation of how this world came to be. They didn't know that only a small fraction of people on earth actually believe in the silly notions of evolution—that fish could change into amphibians, amphibians into lizards, and then eventually lizards into birds.

But now the idea of creation was like an open window to Alexander. It seemed to free him up to express all the things he had ever wanted to say about how foolish the theory of evolution sounded.

"I've always wondered, if monkeys changed into men at one time in history, is it possible for men to change back into monkeys?" he exclaimed.

They all had a good laugh over that one, and Natasha had to admit that sometimes Alexander acted more like a monkey than a man.

Then Leonid told them the story of Eden and how Satan used a snake to deceive Adam and Eve into eating some fruit—how they fell for his deceptions, and how they hid themselves when God came looking for them in the evening. Alexander and Natasha sat in awe when they heard that a lamb had to be sacrificed to represent the Savior who would one day come to save the world from sin. And tears came to Natasha's eyes when she heard that earth's first couple had to leave their garden home. Their sin had cost the human race a life in paradise.

"Why would Adam and Eve take the fruit if God asked them not to?" Natasha wanted to know. "Didn't they have enough to eat?"

Alexander smiled at the innocence of her question, but then he grew sad as he listened to Leonid continue. "Yes, they had enough. God had been so good to them, giving them everything they could possibly desire in their new garden home. But you see, Eve grew curious when she ventured away from Adam, and suddenly she found herself at the tree God had told them not to even visit. She stopped to look and listen to a beautiful serpent talk. She should have been shocked at such a thing, but a talking snake was something she had never seen before. And instead of remembering that God loved her and had given her and Adam so many blessings, she trusted the words of the serpent instead of God."

Leonid shook his head. "I'm afraid we are very much like them today. When we are tempted to do wrong, we usually know what the right thing to do is, but we want to play with sin. Unfortunately, like Eve, we don't understand the power of Satan and how much he hates God. We don't understand that Satan's greatest delight is to make us do wrong, which of course will bring God great pain because He is our Father and loves us so much."

Alexander and Natasha found it hard to believe that evil could become such a dominant force in the world so quickly after the fall of man. They were amazed that God could be so compassionate and patient with generation after generation who turned away from Him to live lives of brutality and lust. As Leonid told them about Noah, it did not surprise them to think that God had to send a flood of waters to destroy a world that was out of control.

Leonid told Natasha and Alexander stories about God's chosen people—stories about Moses, Gideon, and Samuel—and how God used these men to lead His people. He told them stories about leaders like Daniel and Esther who were able to give God's people hope.

"Despite the fact that Adam and Eve sinned, God had a plan," Leonid told them. "His plan was to save the world and bring people back to Him. No sacrifice was too great to accomplish this goal!"

"But how can God save people if they keep wanting to be bad?" Alexander asked. "I mean, people are basically bad." He pointed to a bookshelf on one wall of their tiny apartment. "I have a few books on history there, and from what I've read, history tends to repeat itself. No matter how good a ruler is or how many good things he has done for a country, when he dies, sooner or later a new king or dictator will rise up who is evil and thinks only of himself."

Leonid nodded in agreement. "A very good point, Alexander. You've hit the nail on the head. People do tend to be bad, but it doesn't change the fact that God wants to save us. However, He won't force us to do anything we don't want to do. It's our choice; we have to want to be saved. It's strictly our choice."

Leonid held up his Bible. "People have always had choices. The people before the Flood had a choice whether to go into the ark, or not. It was their choice. The Israelites had a choice about whether they would believe God could take them through the Red Sea when they were trying to escape from the Egyptians. It was their choice. They had to step out in faith or be left behind. God's people had a choice when Samuel said that Israel didn't need a king. Samuel told them that God should be their king, but again, it was their choice. And they chose to get a king of their own anyway."

Alexander and Natasha were torn between asking questions and just sitting and listening to what Leonid was telling them. As he turned the pages of his Bible to show them where all the stories were, they were overwhelmed that all this was in one Book.

There was so much to share, but Leonid knew that Alexander and Natasha had no knowledge of the Bible. How much could he share with them on this first night without overwhelming them? He didn't want to overdo it, but they were just drinking in everything—it didn't seem to really matter what story he was telling them. It was clear to Leonid that the Holy Spirit was doing His job in guiding the discussion.

But when Leonid told them the story of how Jesus came as a baby to save the human race, Alexander and Natasha stopped asking questions. They were silent as they heard that Jesus lived the life of a poor man so that He could give hope to those who had nothing. They were filled with wonder that Jesus brought healing to demoniacs and the deaf and dumb.

The story about Jesus in the garden, facing Satan's temptations alone, was a sad one, and the crucifixion was almost too incredible to believe. They couldn't imagine such cruelty toward anyone, let alone the Creator of the universe.

Alexander and Natasha watched Leonid's face as he talked. They knew they had never seen anyone so godly and so full of peace as Leonid. They could tell he really believed in what he was saying, and that he truly did love this God at the center of all his stories.

The young couple was so interested in the things Leonid was sharing that they forgot all about the time. When they finally looked at their watches, they realized it was already past midnight.

CHAPTER 5

"Oh! Look at the time!" Natasha exclaimed. "We've kept you so late—we're so sorry! You must be tired, Leonid."

"Thank you, but you shouldn't worry, "Leonid smiled again. "I'm used to this. I sell books for a living, and when people want to hear about God's Word, I forget about the time too."

"We must not keep you any longer. Do you live far from here?"

"Not far. About twenty minutes by train."

Alexander got to his feet. "Can you come again soon? We want to hear more." He took Leonid's hand and shook it. "If tonight was this much fun, I can only imagine what the next time will be like."

"Yes, and will you come for supper this time?" Natasha's eyes shone as she looked at Leonid eagerly. "If you eat with us the next time you visit, we can even talk about the books during supper."

"I'd like that." Leonid put the two books back into his bag. "Thank you for a pleasant evening. I look forward to seeing you again soon."

He set his book bag down on the floor. "Before I go I would like to pray to our Father in heaven. The three of us have so much to talk about, and we need the Holy Spirit to help us and guide us when we visit like this."

And so Leonid prayed, and the young Russian couple marveled at the way he spoke to this spiritual Being they couldn't see! Leonid talked to God as though God were right there with them in the room. It was the most moving experience Alexander and Natasha had ever had!

It was a short prayer, and when Leonid finished, he was smiling. "Thank you for a wonderful evening. I look forward to coming again in a few days with your books. You can be sure of that."

The dogs nuzzled up against Leonid as he put on his coat and prepared to leave. He gave Boris and Lexi one more pat on the head, and then went out into the night.

Alexander and Natasha were overjoyed at the good news Leonid called the gospel. It was all so new to them. The kind of books Leonid was selling were rare in Russia at this time because the communist government forbade the making and selling of such books. If Leonid's books should be found by the authorities, they would be confiscated.

And owning such books could jeopardize the status of a person's job, too. People gained and lost jobs because of who they knew and how agreeable they were with local officials. If a person didn't cooperate with government leaders, it was very easy for them to be reassigned to a less prestigious job "somewhere else." Unfortunately, it was that simple.

Natasha's job was not that important, but it did allow her to stay close to home so that she could prepare Alexander's meals, watch the dogs, and keep their house in spotless condition just as she liked it.

Alexander's job was a bit more important financially, and to lose it would be very hard for them. It paid a little bit better than jobs working as a store cashier or street sweeper. He and Natasha needed the money, and they certainly didn't need the attention the KGB might bring if they discovered books in their house like the ones Leonid was selling.

What would happen to them if they were caught with the books? If the books should be considered a serious enough political threat, or if the local officials wanted to make an example of the offender, then the penalty could be much more severe. The owners of such books could be fined and sometimes even imprisoned for a while.

Alexander and Natasha talked about the dangers associated with their newfound knowledge, and together they decided that they didn't care. These two books promised to make a huge impact in their lives. Already the books had brought them a renewed sense of hope and energy for life.

They were worried, however, about the trouble this could make for Leonid if the government found out he was selling Bibles and other religious books in their apartment complex. What would happen to him if he were caught? After all, in most parts of the Soviet Union, it was against the law to have a job other than the one assigned by the local officials. Worse yet, since the government taught students and citizens that there was no God, selling books about Him was illegal and considered a criminal offense.

It was frightening thinking about such things, but it could happen. Unfortunately, they still didn't know God well enough to trust Him, and they didn't know how to pray, but they were learning. As it was, the most they could hope for was that everything would work out for the best so they could get their books.

The angels must have smiled to see this couple so hungry for truth, and they marked the little Russian home for special attention and care. A new day was beginning for Natasha and Alexander, and the angels wanted to be there when the couple gave their hearts to Jesus.

The days passed quickly, with the tasks of life occupying their time. Alexander rode the train to and from the city bank, and Natasha did business from her small windowed office on the first floor of their building. Alexander stood in his usual place near the bank vault, and Natasha kept the halls of the apartment complex looking neat and clean.

Before they knew it, Leonid was knocking on their door several evenings later. The Russian couple could not explain the giddy anticipation they had felt all week at having such a guest in their home. Even Boris and Lexi felt it. Was it the good news of salvation he was bringing them that made their hearts race? Was it the exciting stories from long ago that gave them glimpses of truth and forgiveness and power to live for Jesus? Of course they also knew Leonid was bringing them the two coveted books they had bought, and that had much to do with the excitement in the air.

Once again Alexander and Natasha welcomed Leonid in and made him feel at home. And once again they forgot all about their worries and listened excitedly as Leonid shared with them the keys to happiness and contentment in life. He told them amazing stories from the Bible, but he also shared miracle stories of modern-day people he had met who had been searching for God.

He told them of a little old babushka who had been asking God to send her someone who would help her learn about God. "When I came to her door and knocked on it, the little woman opened the door excitedly. 'Come in! Come in!' her eyes were almost dancing. 'I have been expecting you for several days.' I asked the woman why, and she said she had been praying that God would help her. She did not know much about God, but she knew that He must exist because nothing else made sense. So she prayed, and then she had a dream, and a shining man in her dream told her that someone would come to her house with two books about God. These books would tell her about the soon coming of Jesus from heaven."

CHAPTER 6

Alexander stared at Leonid expectantly. "And the shining man in her dream was coming from God?"

"I am thinking he was," Leonid nodded reverently, "because in her dream the woman saw the two books with their titles in the shining man's hand."

"The very titles?" Alexander's eyes widened.

"The very titles."

"And what were the names of the two books?"

Leonid pulled a copy of the Bible and *The Great Controversy* from his book bag. "These two books."

Natasha gasped. "The very ones you sold us?" A hush of holy silence settled upon the little room in their apartment, and she put her hands to her heart.

"The very ones." Leonid glanced at Natasha and Alexander, letting the impact of his words settle in.

"This is amazing!" Natasha could hardly believe her ears. "Truly this is a miracle straight from heaven. God answered the babushka's prayer in a powerful way, and you are living proof of it, Leonid. We are so privileged to hear this story from a man of God who experienced such a thing!"

"It truly was a miracle," Leonid agreed, "and the woman was so astonished that she began to cry. Over and over again she kept saying 'Slava boag! Slava boag! Praise God! Praise God!'"

"Thank you for this story." Alexander took Leonid's hand. "As you did for this woman, you have brought us hope and a new life to live."

"Praise God! Slava boag!" Leonid humbly replied.

"Slava boag!" Alexander echoed his thoughts.

The three of them studied the Bible some more, and then Leonid said he needed to go visit his mother. "Thank you again, Alexander. Natasha. God bless you both. Now remember, God promises in His holy Bible that we are not to worry. He will care for us."

Leonid held up the Bible he was carrying. "This book says, 'Do not fear, for I am with you. Do not be afraid, for I am your God. I will strengthen you and help you, and I will hold you up with My righteous hand.'"

"We can find these words in our new Bible?" Alexander's eyes brightened again as he held up his own copy of the sacred book.

"You can. It is found in the section called Isaiah. Chapter 41, I believe." He smiled and got down on his knees. "And now, before I go, let us pray to God that He will keep you in the palm of His hand to protect you."

Alexander and Natasha knelt on the big round carpet in the center of their living room. They bowed their heads as Leonid prayed to the God of the universe they were learning to love. "Our Father, thank you so much for guarding our lives every day with your love," Leonid prayed. "We know you care for us because we are your children. Please be with Alexander and Natasha as they begin their journey to your kingdom. Let them always know it is Your Word that can give them the answers they need to live a happy life. Please watch and keep their steps day by day until we see each another again. And come soon to take us home, dear Lord. In Jesus name we pray. Amen."

"I have a special favor to ask of you," Leonid said as he got to his feet. "I'm leaving on the train to Sokolovo tonight, and will not be back for

two days. But I have this box of books with me here that I've been de-
livering today to some of my customers." He picked up the box sitting
on the floor by the kitchen table. "Unfortunately, I've not been able to
deliver them all because some of the people were not home, and now it
is late. I don't have time to take the books back to my apartment before
leaving for the train station." He glanced at his watch. "I must go there
immediately. Is it possible for me to leave the box of books here with
you until I come back from my trip? I will pick them up when I return."

Alexander slapped Leonid on the shoulder. "Of course! We would be
glad to help you out! Anything to help a man of God!"

Leonid breathed a sigh of relief. "Thank you so much! You folks are
such good friends! Now I don't have to hurry on my way to the station."

Alexander reached for the box, "Maybe we'll have time to look over
some of the books before you come back for them." He grinned in his
boyish way, and Natasha laughed.

"I don't think so," she said, as she took the box of books from him
and carried it back to a room that was used for storage. "We'll be too
busy reading the ones we already bought."

And she was right. Each morning before Alexander left, they would
try to squeeze in a few minutes of reading while they ate their breakfast
of eggs, Russian black bread, and kasha, a kind of porridge made from
buckwheat and served warm with sour cream. And then as soon as
Alexander arrived home in the evening, they would hurriedly eat supper and wash the dishes in order to spend as much time as possible with
the books. Even so, they often read late into the night.

"This is all so exciting!" Natasha admitted on the second night of
reading the books together. "Whatever will we do with our time when
we've finished reading the books?"

"That's easy," Alexander laughed. "We'll just read them through
again."

"And again! And again!" Natasha chimed in excitedly.

A peace settled over them as they read together. The next morning Alexander teased Natasha as he left for work. "Now don't be reading snatches of the books while I'm gone today."

"I know! I know!" Natasha retorted with a sweet smile. "We read them together the first time through." She gave him a hug. "That way you can explain things to me from a historical point of view. I never was any good with history."

CHAPTER 7

On Sunday evening the weather was a bit warmer, and to Alexander and Natasha's surprise, Uncle Vitelli and Aunt Marina showed up. Everyone was excited to be together again after being cooped up inside during the long winter. And of course Boris and Lexi were anxious to get in on all the hugs and kisses being spread around. It was a grand evening as the men discussed weather and politics, and the women talked about all the latest gossip.

"Alexander? Natasha? I have an announcement to make!" Uncle Vitelli said with the pomp of a king. "I am thinking of buying an old automobile!"

"An automobile!" Natasha's mouth dropped open in surprise. "Can you afford it? Automobiles are awfully expensive! I don't think I know anyone who owns one."

"I've been saving my money for years," Uncle Vitelli bragged, "and I'm going to get one! Marina does not like the idea so much, but she will when she gets to ride in it!"

"This is news!" Alexander was clearly excited. "Where will you buy it? Does someone have one they will sell? It must clearly be broken if they want to sell it."

"All cars have problems," Uncle Vitelli said with a wave of his hand, as if to dismiss the thought. "It is a small one, and old, but I'm getting it for a very good price. A friend who works at the accounting office of my building said he must sell it."

Alexander listened, his eyebrows up. He was waiting for the inevitable downside of such a deal. Few people in Russia could afford to own a car, so there had to be a catch.

Uncle Vitelli hesitated, and then added with a flourish, "It will not run. It just sits in a storage room where we work, but the building manager said he must get it out of there." Uncle Vitelli gave a triumphant smile. "I have seen it, and it looks nice. I took my nephew with me to inspect it, and he says it needs work, but he will help me fix it if I will let him use it sometimes."

"Well, that much is good," Alexander smiled. "How much does the car cost?"

"Six hundred rubles."

"Six hundred rubles? I wish I had that much money," Alexander confessed. "I would not spend it on an automobile, though."

"No? And what would you spend it on?"

"I don't know. Traveling, maybe. Good books. Books can take you anywhere, and they cost less than the actual trip, you know."

Uncle Vitelli smiled. "Ah yes, I love to read, but riding in an automobile down the road on a nice spring day is much better than reading about someone doing it."

"You make your point well," Alexander laughed.

By now Natasha and Marina had gone back to subjects of more interest to women, like the price of beets in the market, and where they could get a new pair of hose, and where Aunt Viktoriya had been getting her hair dyed.

But the dogs were getting excited again. Boris grabbed one of his toys in his mouth and begged for Uncle Vitelli to play fetch with him. Then he jumped up on Aunt Marina's armchair and began barking so loudly that no one could hear themselves talk.

"Oh, Boris! Get down!" Alexander scolded him. "Is that any way to treat our guests? Shame on you! Natasha, let's put the dogs into the back room. They will be quiet there, and then we can have some peace and quiet."

"That's a good idea!" Natasha turned to her aunt and uncle. "We're so sorry! We should have done that a long time ago. Boris is just a puppy still, and he's always getting into everything! The rascal! He chews up everything he can find! When Lexi had her last litter of puppies, we gave them all away, but somehow we became attached to this one."

She rubbed the fur on Boris' neck and scratched him under the chin, all the while giving him baby talk. "Come on, you big puppy dog! You are such a big, noisy, clumsy dog! But we love you anyway, yes we do!" She took him by the collar, and led the two dogs to the back of the apartment. "Now come in here awhile, and be a good dog, Boris! Come on now! Be a good dog!" she said, pushing him into the storage room. "Stay with your mother here where you belong."

For the first time that evening it was quiet.

The two ladies then prepared a warm supper, and what a sumptuous meal it was. Bright red borsch made from beets and cabbage and carrots. Thick slices of Russian bread, slabs of goat cheese imported from the Baltic region, and of course the usual tea offered at every Russian meal. For dessert Natasha brought out one of her famous prianieki cakes.

"Speaking of books," Alexander said, getting back to the discussion from before supper, "we just bought two new ones the other day."

"New books?" Uncle Vitelli raised his eyebrows. "What kind?"

"Books about history. Religion. The future."

"You'd really like them, Uncle Vitelli," Natasha got in on the conversation now, her eyes lighting up. "Especially the one that talks about religious history."

"That good, huh?"

"Absolutely! We can't put it down. The book starts out with the history of the Jews in the Roman Empire during the first century AD. Then it goes on through the later history of the Roman Empire. Right now we're reading about the renaissance and reformation in Europe during the 1500s."

"Hmmm, what's the name of the book?"

"It's called *The Great Controversy*."

CHAPTER 8

Alexander let Natasha tell Uncle Vitelli all about the book. She would do a better job of getting him interested than Alexander ever could. Uncle Vitelli was sometimes too contrary for his own good. He would argue sometimes, just to be argue, it seemed.

"Let's have a look." Uncle Vitelli really sounded interested now. "*The…Great… Controversy*," he slowly read. He thumbed through the book and began reading from a couple of the chapters. "This looks very interesting," he said after a few minutes.

"We love it!" Natasha said. "Here, let me read you a part we found really interesting." Natasha reached for the book. "It's over here in the chapter about the Waldenses." She turned the pages quickly, and then finally stopped and ran her finger down to a specific paragraph.

It says here, "Behind the lofty bulwarks of the mountains, in all ages the refuge of the persecuted and oppressed, the Waldenses found a hiding place. Here the light of truth was kept burning amid the darkness of the Middle Ages. Here for a thousand years, witnesses for the truth maintained the ancient faith."

"Waldenses, huh? So, who were these people hiding from anyway?" Uncle Vitelli asked.

"Church leaders. Government politicians," Alexander grew serious. "People who didn't believe exactly like they did."

Uncle Vitelli looked over the top of his horn-rimmed glasses. "That would be serious stuff. I mean, having to hide from everybody just so you could live like you wanted to? I'd hate it."

Alexander frowned and lowered his voice. "I think we've all been there."

"So, now? Where did you say you got the book?"

"Well, actually that's the most interesting part of all," Natasha beamed. "A young book salesman brought us the books. He knows all about religious history, and he can quote long passages from his books." Natasha held up the other book Leonid had sold them. "This book here is the oldest book in the world. It's called the Bible. Some of it was written 1400 years BC."

"Leonid read to us from the book, and it has some of the most incredible stories we've ever heard," Alexander joined in. "Stories that defy the imagination, and they're all true."

"Leonid, huh?" Uncle Vitelli reached for the Bible.

"That's right. He said that the Bible has lots of critics, but every year archeological discoveries are made that prove more and more of the stories to be historically accurate."

"Like?" Uncle Vitelli stared over the top of his glasses again.

"Like a story about a worldwide flood. Noah's flood, they called it." Alexander stared at Uncle Vitelli. "You'd like that one. It's at the beginning of a book called Genesis. It has to do with the scientific world and all. Here—we marked some of them. See for yourself." He opened the holy book and pointed to the chapter with the story.

"And there's a story about a man who could tell the future through dreams." Natasha leaned over Uncle Vitelli's shoulder. "He helped save ancient Egypt and all the other Mediterranean countries from starvation."

Uncle Vitelli flipped the pages of the Bible. "I see you've marked all kinds of stories here." He paused and began to read, "So the people shouted when the priests blew the trumpets. And it happened when the people heard the sound of the trumpet, and the people shouted with a great shout, that the wall fell down flat." Uncle Vitelli paused as if deep in thought. "Did that really happen?" he asked, a funny expression on his face.

"According to Leonid, the book salesman, yes."

Uncle Vitelli turned over some more pages and began reading again.

"God is our refuge and strength, a very present help in trouble. Therefore we will not fear, even though the earth be removed, and though the mountains be carried into the midst of the sea; though its waters roar and be troubled, though the mountains shake with its swelling."

He closed the book and looked at the cover, still holding his finger in the spot where he had been reading. "I've heard this book is on some kind of contraband list." He glanced at Natasha, and then Alexander.

"We thought of that," Alexander said slowly, "but it's so interesting, and it doesn't really say anything against the USSR. The book doesn't even mention it."

"Hmmm," Uncle Vitelli shrugged. "Looks good to me." He raised his eyebrows. "I like the books. When you're done with them, send them on over."

CHAPTER 9

The next morning dawned bright and clear. Not a cloud was in the sky as Alexander got up and prepared for the new day. While he put on his uniform for work, Natasha made their breakfast. It was a simple one that they ate nearly every day of the week—more kasha with sour cream on it, and some potatoes. It was not a meal for a king, but it was what they could afford. Alexander would have liked some sausage to go with it, but sausage was expensive, and he didn't always know whether he could trust it. When they did eat it, Natasha usually had to re-cook it to make sure any bacteria or sickness in it was killed.

"Have some more potatoes," Natasha yawned sleepily. "Watch out, now! The pan is hot!"

"Mmmm! They smell so good," Alexander reached for a second helping. "Thank you, dear."

She stared at her husband, handsome in his gray uniform. "God is good," she smiled sweetly. "I think our life is changed forever. Ever since Leonid's visit, it is like there is nothing that can go wrong. It is as if the peace of God is in our hearts, and nothing can take it away." She rubbed her eyes awake.

"That's exactly what I was thinking." Alexander patted Natasha on the cheek. "It seems too good to be true, doesn't it?"

They read a few pages from their books, and then Alexander suddenly pushed himself back from the table. "I'd better take the dogs for a short walk before I leave."

Natasha got a startled look in her eye. "That's right! I totally forgot about Boris and Lexi! They've been so quiet! We never let them out of the back room last night after Uncle Vitelli and Aunt Marina left! Get your coat, Alexander. I'll let them out right now."

She hurried to the back room, talking to Alexander as she went. "I thought it was odd when the dogs didn't wake me up this morning. Boris is no small dog. I hope he's been a good boy. He must be ready for a good run by now! Come Boris! Here Lexi!" she called as she opened the door to the storeroom and turned on the light.

And then Alexander heard her gasp. "Oh, no! You naughty dogs!" she half shrieked. "Boris! What have you done! Oh, Alexander!" she called in alarm. "This is terrible! It cannot be!"

By now Alexander had rushed to the back room to find Natasha standing speechless in the middle of the room. Boris was running about excitedly, his tail wagging, while Lexi looked up at Natasha with pleading eyes. Strewn everywhere were things that had been on some shelves in the storeroom. Two or three dishes lay broken on the floor, and holes had been chewed in a warm winter coat.

But the sight that horrified Alexander and Natasha the most was the box of books that Leonid had left with them. The box had been knocked off a small table in the room, and was on its side on the floor. Bibles and books had been dragged out by the dogs and scattered across the floor. Pages lay everywhere, torn from the wonderful books. Teeth marks scarred the pages and bindings, and some of the book covers were gnawed beyond recognition.

"This cannot be!" Natasha moaned, sinking to her knees. "The dogs have eaten the Bibles! They have chewed them to bits! Oh, Alexander! What will we do?"

Boris and Lexi tried to make their peace with Natasha, but she pushed them away. "You naughty, naughty dogs! Don't you try and be all sweet now!" she scolded them angrily. "How could you have done this? I should give you a horrible spanking!"

"We should never have left the dogs in here so long!" Alexander groaned, his hand on his head and his shoulders sagging. "We were talking and talking last night and forgot all about them." He closed his eyes in exasperation. "Whatever will we say to Leonid?"

"All his wonderful books!" Natasha bowed her head in shame. "Gone! Destroyed! Look at the pages all ripped out! Torn from the books and laying all around like this!"

"And all the teeth marks! They look as if a wild animal has torn them to bits!"

Natasha's eyes finally softened a bit as she looked at Boris, his face the picture of innocence. "Oh, Alexander! Boris didn't know he was doing wrong! He's just a puppy!"

"But he ruined the books, and now we are going to have to pay for them!" Alexander's eyes flashed angrily. "You bad, bad dogs!" he said coldly.

Natasha glanced around her. "How many books were in the box, Alexander?"

He sighed tiredly and knelt down beside her. "I don't know, Tash. Let's see, it looks like this is part of one, and this piece here goes with it. And this must be another." He bent down, "And here's another. Four, five... six... seven... no, that could be part of this one over here."

"Eight... nine," Natasha began counting with him, "ten... eleven... Oh, Alexander, there must be over a dozen books damaged here." She covered her face with her hands.

"And they were God's books, ready to do so much good, to bring the gospel to many people in this big city." Alexander slowly rose to his feet, shaking his head dejectedly. What could they say? The ruined books had been promised to customers who had already paid for them. Now the people would have to wait even longer for their books.

But the thing Alexander and Natasha feared the most was the look they knew they would see on Leonid's face when they told him the sad news. He had been so good to bring them the hope of a new life with God, and this was how they were repaying him?

"Go ahead and take the dogs for their morning run," Natasha said sadly, still on her knees among the scattered pages and fragments of the books on the floor. "I'll take care of this mess."

The dogs scampered away at mention of a walk, suddenly oblivious to the carnage they had left behind.

As Alexander walked the sidewalks though the local park watching Boris and Lexi run playfully, he wished he could be as carefree as them. But he knew that wasn't possible. The ruined books loomed before him like a giant immovable mountain.

Alexander picked up a stick and threw it for the dogs to chase. The last few hours had turned out to be a disaster! A catastrophe! Just the evening before, he and Natasha had been sharing with Uncle Vitelli and Aunt Marina the wonderful new books that had come to bless their lives!

And now this. In all his years of living, he couldn't remember anything that had ever turned out quite as bad! It seemed a calamity of astronomical proportions. The books would cost an incredible amount of money to replace, but it was more than that. There was something more that was bothering him beyond the obvious. Maybe it was because of what the books represented. They were religious books—books that had a real purpose and had been prepared especially to take the good news of salvation to the world. The tragedy was almost sacrilegious in a strange sort of way, a desecration of something holy. He didn't know much about the history behind the books, how they had been written, or what it had taken to get them printed and smuggled into

Novosibirsk. But one thing was sure—God Himself was involved here.

Alexander remembered Leonid's story about the lady who had prayed and how an angel appeared to her in a dream, telling her to look for a man with two books. In his mind, that made them holy books. And were the rest of Leonid's books any less holy? Alexander thought not, and that made his situation all the more desperate. The thought that Boris and Lexi had chewed up Leonid's books seemed worse than irreverence. It was like a slap in the face of God.

CHAPTER 10

I must be strong, at least for Natasha, he reasoned as he walked back to the apartment, trying to shake off the tangle of thoughts that threatened to overrun his mind. He was very quiet when he stepped back into the warmth of their little apartment, but he had a determined look on his face. "Don't worry," he assured Natasha. "We'll think of a way to raise the money to pay for the books."

Alexander and Natasha sat down at the kitchen table to ponder what they should do next. They looked through the box of books once again to survey the damage. Out of the twenty-some books in the box, fourteen of them were ruined beyond repair.

"Whatever will we say to Leonid?" There were tears in Natasha's eyes." God sent him to us with such a wonderful message, and this is how we repay him?"

"We will just have to pay for the books, that's all."

"Yes, of course, but they will cost so much. How can we ever find the money to do this?"

Alexander gave a deep tired sigh. "I don't know, Natasha, but we must. It is only right."

The day had hardly begun, but already Natasha thought he looked tired. She bowed her head in submission to the problem they must face.

"Maybe you're right."

"God will help us." Alexander put his head in his hands. "It was not really our fault. The devil was here to give us trouble."

"You think so?

"I'm sure of it. The devil does not want us to be happy. He doesn't want us to know about God or the truth from His holy Bible."

Natasha's eyes grew wide as though she suddenly understood for the first time. "So the devil is mad at us, and he made Boris do it!" She turned to Boris who sat looking at her warily. "So that's it, Boris! Did you hear that? You should not have helped Satan destroy the good books, you naughty dog! Shame on you!" She shook her finger at him, and then glanced at the mother dog. "And Lexi! You should have made your puppy behave!"

"What's done is done," Alexander shook his head grimly. "We will just have to tell Leonid the truth when he comes. I just hope he understands. But God will have to help us," he added, "if such a thing is possible. We cannot pay for the books now. God will have to help us somehow find the money for these books."

He got up from the table, his coat still on. "Now I must go to work. We must pray to God, Natasha, like Leonid did. Maybe God will help us find a way to pay for these books. We can talk about it tonight when I come home."

Alexander left the apartment and made his way to the train station, where he boarded the train that would take him to the business district. He stared out the window of the slow moving train. The click-clack of the wheels on the rails punctuated his thoughts as he passed by high-rise apartments, through darkened subway tunnels, and finally above the busy streets in the town's business section where he worked.

What a dilemma he was in! Alexander closed his eyes and tried to think of a solution. The thought of all those books lying around torn to shreds was ominous. How was he going to pay for the books the dogs had ruined? He was a poor man. He mentally calculated how much the books would cost to replace, and the thought of such a thing seemed financially impossible! He had already given Leonid all the money they had in the house to pay for the two books they bought. That had been the money they needed to pay for food and medicine for the rest of the month. Alexander wouldn't receive his monthly salary for another two weeks.

Fortunately, Alexander's job did not require him to concentrate much, because he was certainly doing a poor job of that this morning. The gated area where the vaults were located was a quiet, expansive room with little traffic most hours of the day. There was plenty of time to think about the trouble he and Natasha had gotten themselves into. Maybe too much time.

All morning Alexander couldn't shake the feeling of dread that had started their day. As he stood at his post by the bank vault, he tried to think of what he would say or do if he were in Leonid's shoes listening to a customer tell him that the books he had trusted to their care were ruined. He couldn't imagine the situation turning out very well. After all, was there any really good way to say, "Oh, by the way, our dogs ate your books?"

He tried praying, but his prayers seemed to go no higher than the ornately tiled ceiling stretching over him in the quietness of the bank antechambers. Finally, he bowed his head and laid his anxieties before God. "I have no answers," he prayed. "Lord, only You can help us get past this horrible disaster! Who knows? Maybe there is even a reason You allowed such a thing to happen. Didn't I hear Leonid say once that everything always turns out for the best when you work for God?"

Alexander smiled inwardly, though his face betrayed him otherwise. Of course, such a thing couldn't be entirely true at face value, but something in his heart told him he would rather be a poor man and have peace with God, than have things the other way around.

Meanwhile, back in the apartment Natasha was trying to put the torn and ragged pages back into the books, but it was no use. Most of the books were ruined beyond repair! Hundreds of pages were ripped and shredded and wet with dog drool, and the book covers were full of teeth marks! She felt terrible! As she looked at the hopeless mess, she knew there was absolutely nothing she could do! There was nothing anyone could do! And there was no one to talk to about it either, not that it would have mattered much. The whole thing was too depressing for words. Even Boris looked sad at the turn of events.

All that day Natasha thought about the Bibles and books. Often she would stop her work to wipe the tears from her eyes. *It's bad enough that the books are ruined,* Natasha thought. *Books are precious to the people of Russia—they're like old friends. Books are to be read and reread, and then shared with others. But these books are God's books. They've been printed to bring the gospel to people searching for God. They were entrusted to us for safe keeping, and they were very expensive! What are we going to do about it?*

At one point during the morning she literally fell to her knees and prayed tearfully, almost desperately. "Please, God, we didn't mean to ruin the books. We are so glad you sent Leonid to us, but we're just sick about the dogs tearing the books all up! Please help us find a way to pay for them!" And then almost as an afterthought she stammered, "I don't really know You, God. Leonid says You are the God of the universe, and yet You care about us. Please God, if You will, I know You can help us find a way!"

Somehow praying seemed to help, though she had never really prayed alone before. Her prayers gave her courage to wipe the tears from her eyes and continue on with her work. And working helped some, forcing her mind to focus on other things. However, by the time Alexander came home that night, Natasha was exhausted from her long day of worrying and anxious prayer.

CHAPTER 11

O h, Alexander," she rushed to meet him at the door, "I'm so glad you're home! I thought this day would never end!" She hugged him tightly as if having him there would make all their problems go away. "I've been worrying all day and even praying some like you said, but I'm sick at heart!" She stared almost frantically into his eyes. "Have you thought of a way that we can get the money to pay for the books?"

"I have not." Alexander hung his head dejectedly. "But I prayed too," his eyes brightened a bit, "and I know everything will turn out okay. It has too." He sighed as he took off his coat. "We have the new books and the truth they have brought us, and we have each other. That is worth more than anything, don't you think?"

"Yes," Natasha looked hopeful for the first time that day. "I guess you're right."

"And we will find a way to pay for the books, as long as Leonid is willing to wait for the money." He looked confidently at his pretty little wife. "And I've thought of something else. If we have to pay for the books, we'll own them. Who knows? Maybe God will do something special with these books anyway."

Natasha looked at him, her face a puzzle of perplexity, but then she smiled and gave his broad shoulders another hug. "I believe that is possible. Didn't we read with Leonid somewhere in the holy Bible that with God all things are possible?"

The sun was going down now, and its last shafts of golden light were streaming through the kitchen window. For a few minutes the warmth of the kitchen and the quietness of the moment captured something special for the young Russian couple. They knew that Leonid might come that night for his books—in fact, he might come any moment now—but it no longer frightened them as it had earlier that morning. They still did not have a game plan, but the peace of God was in their home, so it seemed that nothing else mattered.

And then suddenly there was someone knocking at the door, and they knew it had to be Leonid. The moment of truth had come, and they both looked at one other as if to gather strength.

"Oh, Alexander! He's here already?" Natasha's eyes suddenly grew frantic again. "What will we tell him?"

Alexander reached for the door. "If it's him, we've got to tell him the truth, and we must do it now. Let's get it over with!"

The door swung open, and there in the doorway was Leonid again, the handsome young salesman. "Alexander! Natasha! It's so good to see you!" he smiled. "How have you been? I've thought of you all this week, and have been looking forward to our time together again."

Boris and Lexi were overjoyed to see Leonid. Boris jumped up on him as though he had always been a member of the family. Leonid was grinning like a school boy, and it unnerved Alexander to see him so happy. He couldn't help but wonder how Leonid would feel when they told him the truth about the books.

"We've been waiting for you to return too!" Alexander tried to cover his true feelings. "Come in! It's so good to see you! How was your trip on the train?"

"God is good! The trip was a safe one. My mother has not been feeling well during the last few months, but now, praise God, she is doing much better. My pastor came to visit her, and we prayed and anointed her to help her get well." A look of holy peace was on Leonid's face.

Alexander thought about what Leonid was saying. They had anointed his mother? Whatever that was, it sounded interesting, but he fought against his curiosity. There would be plenty of time for that later. Right now he just wanted to get the news about the ruined books out in the open. Before any more small talk or the usual cup of tea could be used to mask the truth, Alexander wanted to speak his mind. This was important! It had taken enough hours of happiness and peace from them already!

"Leonid, please sit down," Alexander urged his guest before he could lose the courage to say what he needed to say. "We have some bad news for you. We..." Alexander tried to collect his wits. "This is a very hard thing to tell you, Leonid. But it is..."

Natasha could stand the awkward strain no longer, and to Leonid's surprise, she suddenly burst into tears.

CHAPTER 12

Leonid could tell that something was terribly wrong, but in spite of Alexander and Natasha's anxiety, he really had no idea what it might be. Was one of them sick? Had they committed a crime or something? Natasha was sobbing so hard he could barely make out the words, but it began to dawn on him what she was trying to say, as one by one the horrible details came out.

"Oh, Leonid! The dogs have torn your lovely box of books all to shreds. They have eaten them all up and destroyed them. We are so sorry! We've thought about how, about how…" And then she burst into tears all over again.

The book salesman just sat there, a kind expression on his face. He looked at them with such compassion and sympathy that Alexander thought he had not understood what Natasha had said.

Alexander stared at Leonid, his eyes ringed with sadness. "Last night our relatives came over for supper," he said, "and we put the dogs into the back room because they would not keep quiet. And we left them in there all night by accident." He glanced at Natasha and hung his head. "It's the same room where we put your books when you left, and we forgot all about them, and the dogs got into the box of books and destroyed them. We were so angry at the dogs," he added, "but there was nothing we could do about it!"

It was so sad to hear the story as it came rushing out, but Leonid never missed a beat as he listened. "You say the dogs ate them up?"

"Chewed them all up!" Natasha joined in again. "And ripped them and destroyed them! It's such a shame!" she sniffed. "They were wonderful books from God! We cannot tell you how sorry we are, and now we must pay for them! It is the only right thing to do!"

Leonid's heart was touched by the young couple's confession. "Natasha? Alexander?" he smiled. "You are right. This is bad news for us, but it's not bad news for God. God owns all the books in the world!

If He has allowed Boris and Lexi to ruin the books, then that's His business! He'll take care of this in His own way."

But Natasha wasn't so sure. She sniffed again through her tears and then glanced down at Boris and Lexi who were lying quietly under the table. "Boris! You naughty dog!" she snapped. "You shouldn't have eaten the books! And Lexi! You were no help!"

The dogs averted their eyes and pressed their bodies and noses close to the floor. It was as if they understood what she was saying, and were trying to keep a low profile because of it.

"OK, OK, they were naughty," Leonid smiled sheepishly, "but—well, come now, Natasha—God loves His creatures too. He made Boris and Lexi, you know. They only did what was natural. You must not be so upset with them, or yourselves for that matter."

He laid his hand on Alexander's shoulder. "We cannot always blame ourselves when things do not go as planned. Remember, people are more important than things, even if it is holy books we're talking about." He reached down and patted Boris on the head. "God is a God of miracles. He is not limited by our earthly troubles. Just our faith."

Leonid began to tell the couple more stories from the Bible where God turned disasters into miracles. He told the story about how God used ten plagues to help the Israelites escape Egyptian slavery, and the miracle of how they walked through the Red Sea on dry land. He told them about Daniel who was thrown into a den of lions because he refused to dishonor God, but that God shut the lion's mouths. He told them stories about the miracles Jesus did to free people from Satan's horrible power.

Natasha and Alexander stared at Leonid, their eyes and ears unbelieving. Who was this young man? Really? Who was he? His name was Leonid, and he was a Christian book salesman, but who was he, really? How could he just forgive them like that? How could he forget that their dogs had destroyed more than a dozen holy books written and dedicated to the spreading of the gospel? They knew now that this must indeed be a holy man of God, ready to stand by them in their hour of need.

They could see that Leonid really did believe in the power of God. They could see the conviction of faith in his eyes and that this setback with the ruined books did not frustrate him in the slightest. It was truly amazing, and it helped convince them that maybe God was not upset with them for the damaged books either.

Then they all bowed their heads as Leonid prayed that all things would work together for the best, that God would take care of the ruined books and bless them all in spite of what had happened.

When he had finished praying, Natasha voiced her thoughts, that Satan might have been a part of what had happened to the books. "Leonid? We were wondering? Is it possible the devil does not want these books to be sold." She raised her eyebrows expectantly. "And because of this he might have made the dogs do such a thing?"

Leonid smiled at her. "This is possible—absolutely possible. And I think it is probably the main reason the dogs ruined the books. Satan does not want these good books to be read because they bring the truth of salvation to those who have them and read them."

Natasha's eyes were still sad, but Leonid could tell she was beginning to relax a bit.

"Bring me the books," Leonid finally asked. "Maybe it is not all as bad as you say it is. Maybe something can be done to fix them after all."

Natasha looked at Leonid, her eyes as big as saucers. "Oh, no, Leonid! There is nothing that can be done for the books!" she insisted. "They are totally destroyed!"

"Alright, then, Boris and Lexi, let's see what you've done?" Leonid looked sternly at the dogs.

Natasha shook her head, and then went to a closet in the hallway and brought out the box of books. "See, even the box is chewed a little bit," she said, as she set it on the kitchen table and began opening the cardboard flaps. Her eyes were still red and puffy from all her crying. "We put all the pieces of the torn books inside. It's such a shame, because…"

But suddenly she let out a gasp. "Alexander? What has happened here?

How can this be?" she exclaimed as she stared into the box. "I can't believe my eyes!"

Alexander and Leonid jumped up and came to look in the box too. "This is impossible!" Natasha kept exclaiming. "It's impossible!"

And indeed it was!

CHAPTER 13

The look of shock on Natasha's face was truly astonishing. At first she and Alexander just stared into the box, but then Alexander began taking the books out of the box one by one. To their amazement, not a book was marked. No pages had teeth marks on them, and the pages were all still in the books as though they had never been out of place. Natasha and Alexander just stood there dumbfounded.

"It's a miracle! It's a miracle!" Alexander repeated over and over. "They were all torn and shredded! They were ruined!" He kept looking at Leonid. "There were teeth marks here, Leonid! I promise you! There were lots of pages out of these books! How can this be?"

"It's true!" Natasha whispered. "The books were all chewed and eaten. Where did they go! We saw them! Over a dozen books were destroyed, and they were in this very box!"

Leonid was smiling by now. He looked from Alexander to Natasha and back to Alexander again.

"No really!" Alexander protested in disbelief and awe, as he watched the expression on Leonid's face. "We saw the books with our own eyes! We did! Just this morning they were in the back room, torn up and ragged! Pieces were everywhere, and we tried to pick them up as best we could and put them back together!"

Natasha nodded. "And we were so angry at the dogs. Boris is still such a puppy, but we felt horrible about what they had done. We were so worried about what we would say to you, and—and..."

Leonid just kept smiling. "God has provided for you," he finally said. "God has heard your prayers, Alexander and Natasha, because you called on Him. He has rewarded your faith in His power because you trusted in Him."

"He has! He has!" Alexander exclaimed in joyful reverence as he stared at the books again, and then he took Natasha's hands in his. "Oh, Natasha! How can we ever doubt God's power again! This is a miracle straight from God's throne in heaven!" He bowed his head. "God knew we could not fix the books ourselves, so He must have sent His angels to put these books back together again!"

Natasha stared at her husband. "It's true!" Her lips began to tremble again. "God and His angels have watched over us. They have come to our home and blessed us with help from heaven. Slava boag!" She sank to the kitchen floor on her knees again, a look of sweet reverence on her face. Leonid and Alexander knelt beside her and bowed their heads in reverence at the incredible miracle so clearly demonstrated on their behalf.

Boris and Lexi didn't know what to do, but the deep significance of the moment was not lost on them. They lay down, put their heads on the floor between their paws, and waited in silence too.

"Lord God of our Fathers," Leonid prayed. "We kneel in awe before You tonight. You are faithful, Lord, and Your mercies are new every morning. Thank you for this amazing miracle that has restored the wonderful books the devil wanted to destroy. How can we thank you for such a gift? I pray that we will never doubt You again for the kindness You have shown us this day."

It wasn't a long prayer, but it was certainly a prayer of thanksgiving for the wonderful miracle God had performed. That God had intervened and restored the books was clear. That He had done it in a profound way so that none could doubt otherwise was unquestionable.

And then Alexander prayed too in his own simple way. God in His mercy had sent His angels from heaven to put the books back together again, and Alexander could only give credit where credit was due. It was the first time he could say he had seen a miracle of supernatural proportions, and his prayer was his testimony.

When they finally rose to their feet, Natasha wiped the tears from her eyes again. "We will never forget this day as long as we live, Leonid! You brought us the Word of God. The devil tried to snatch it away, but God's angels brought it back again!"

And then she looked down at the two dogs. "Boris and Lexi!" she said as she lovingly patted their heads. "Maybe you aren't as naughty as we thought. You decided that the Word of God was good for you too, so you ate the Bibles for breakfast."

"Bibles for breakfast?" Leonid laughed. "Now that's a new one for me!"

And then they all laughed, and Boris and Lexi ran around and around the kitchen table, barking as though they understood perfectly.

BREAD FROM HEAVEN

CHAPTER 1

It was a warm evening. Spring was well on its way in the town of Cahul, and Pastor Sergei Petrovich was glad to see it come. Spring was his favorite time of year with its famous blooming orchards and rows and rows of grape vineyards.

Dusk had come, trading daylight for darkness. Sweet-smelling lilac bushes were already in bloom, their fragrance wafting in through the open window of the small house Sergei shared with his wife, Lena. Near the open window, crickets were tuning up to accompany a warbler singing an evening sonnet.

Sergei sat reading in an overstuffed chair, pouring over Bible passages in preparation for the message he was scheduled to give on Sabbath morning. He adjusted his reading glasses, glanced at the chime clock on the wall, and then at his pretty wife, Lena, who sat opposite of him in the small room of their cozy home. It was almost time for him to leave for one of his secret meetings with the church leaders. Tonight they would be electing a new conference president for the church in the country of Moldova. The leaders always kept the meetings secret so the Communist government wouldn't know the church's business.

Up until a day or two before each meeting, no one ever really knew when or where the meetings were to be held. And with good reasons. If an announcement for an upcoming meeting was broadcasted too many days before the meeting, it often had a way of getting back to KGB headquarters.

Instead, the message was usually sent out strategically through the social grapevine. The pastor's wives would share the information quietly with one another at the farmer's market, or maybe when they visited in groups to make quilts. Then again, sometimes the pastors would go for walks together in the evenings so they could talk. That was how the grapevine operated, and it worked pretty well for church business.

But none of these tricks could deter the KGB indefinitely. On many occasions Sergei had been stopped on the street by KGB officials and asked where and when the next secret conference meeting was going to be held. Of course, Sergei could always answer that he didn't know where, because honestly he didn't. Generally speaking, it was common knowledge that what he didn't know couldn't be used against him.

Interestingly enough, in spite of all the KGB did to threaten Moldovan Christians, from time to time the Soviet government still made public announcements about human rights that were outrageous—like the one that said all Moldovans were guaranteed freedom of religion and worship.

According to the law, church members could meet to worship as long as it was during daylight hours. Such worship services were considered open meetings. This meant that on any given Sabbath KGB spies were apt to show up to observe everyone and everything that went on at the worship services.

It wasn't surprising, then, that the KGB did not like it when secret meetings were held to elect new church leaders. They liked to be in control, and because of this they were a thorn in the side of the church, always watching for a chance to catch the conference board in one of its secret sessions.

They knew that the board was made up of conference officials, and most importantly, pastors. They knew that the board met at least three times a year, and that it always worked at night. To get inside information about when a meeting might be held was their main goal, and they were always trying to bribe members to serve as informers.

But a sacred respect for God's work seemed to pervade the church in Moldova and its capitol, Kishinev. It appeared that everyone, both Christians and non-Christians alike, had too much reverence for the church to serve as an informer or traitor. God had always blessed the local Adventist churches, and fortunately the KGB had never been successful at pulling off one of their sting operations.

And now just that morning Lena had brought word home that it was time for another secret meeting with the church leaders. This time they would be meeting at the home of a believer who was a member of a small local church company. The home had been especially chosen because the leaders felt it was the least likely place a KGB officer would look. It was a very small house on the outskirts of Cahul, off any main roads or streets.

The agenda for the late-night meeting was to discuss evangelism in the country of Moldova and then elect a new president of the church organization there. This was pretty important business for a church that was legally operating in broad daylight, but secretly working underground because they knew how the communist government really felt about their organization.

They had no other choice. A double standard was obviously being practiced by the government, and the KGB was playing dirty. Government officials said nice things about Seventh-day Adventists in public meetings or when they visited as guests in their churches. They always talked about how much they wanted to cooperate with church leaders, but behind the scenes the KGB were forever planning a strategy that would undermine the effectiveness of the church.

Other local Christian churches had also suffered under the notorious hand of the KGB. Some groups reported severe treatment that bordered on downright oppression. It was common for KGB officers to be hard-hearted and even cruel sometimes in their tactics, especially if they didn't live in the local area. One such officer had been nicknamed Ivan the Terrible. A common trick he used was to send spies to mix with the members and find out where scheduled secret meetings would be held. Then later he and his henchmen would suddenly show up with baseball bats and dogs to break up the meeting.

But God had blessed the Adventist congregations and the pastors that served them. Up to now they had always managed to meet undetected. No one could even remember a time when the KGB had been successful in breaking up a secret meeting. Sergei knew it was partly because the Adventists were respected and had few enemies. They always did so much good in the community.

For instance, when there was an epidemic of sickness in a town or village, it was the Seventh-day Adventists who always knew what to do. They had natural remedies and treatments that seemed to work like magic.

And the Adventists were a quiet people. They didn't interfere with the politics of local governments, but instead busied themselves with helping others and spreading a message of hope. And although it was forbidden to hold public meetings for evangelism purposes, everyone knew what the Adventists stood for and who to go to if they had questions about God.

Sergei got up from his chair and went to put on his shoes—it was time for the secret rendezvous. He smiled to himself as he noticed his home's cozy surroundings.

Lena was an excellent housekeeper and kept the place looking spotless. The rooms in the snug little home always had a fresh look about them with everything in its place. The kitchen was always immaculate. Good smells of fresh baked bread or cakes greeted him when he came home in the evening, and Lena always had such nice looking tablecloths spread on the supper table.

And the floors were always so clean. Sergei understood that not wearing his shoes around the house was one of the reasons why. It was the custom in Russian homes to leave the shoes at the door, and Lena saw to it that everyone followed the rule. But what man with a wife like Lena could complain?

Sergei gave his wife a kiss and stepped out into the night. Darkness had fully come, and with it the shadows. That was good since he would certainly need to avoid detection by the KGB. He couldn't afford to have anyone getting suspicious about where he was going.

CHAPTER 2

The night was cool, making the evening walk invigorating. Sergei wondered where exactly the KGB spies were tonight. Did they know of the secret conference meeting being held to elect a new conference president? Were they already following him? Would they crash the meeting and arrest everyone?

So many questions, but Sergei knew what he had to do in the event there was trouble. If he at all suspected someone was following him, he would simply pretend he was going for an evening stroll, and then eventually make his way back home.

As Sergei walked briskly up the street, he thought about the life he led as a pastor. Times were hard in Cahul, and like everyone, he and Lena were feeling the pinch of financial stress. The members in Sergei's churches could not afford to give him much. They could hardly make ends meet themselves, let alone contribute to his salary.

But God is good, Sergei thought. That was the theme of his life, and he wore it like a smile. He was truly a man of God, always giving, always ready to lend a helping hand, and always a man of prayer. His parishioners loved him and looked to him for guidance and spiritual mentoring.

As Sergei neared the house where they were meeting, he slowed his steps and glanced about him in the darkness for telltale signs of a KGB informer. No one under a street lamp. No agents standing on the sidewalk smoking a cigarette in the shadows. He couldn't afford to take any chances.

To be doubly sure, Sergei passed the house and kept right on going. He continued on down the street, turned left at the corner, and then went nonchalantly down another side street. Finally, he circled around and came back by another route.

But there was no one in sight. Sergei smiled to himself in the darkness. God had again helped the leaders to disguise the whereabouts of the meeting. From all appearances, it did seem that all would be well.

After a few more glances into the shadows, Sergei finally felt safe enough to relax. Evidently there was no one out there after all. The KGB had missed the mark again.

Sergei went around to the back of the house and rapped softly on the door using a secret pre-arranged knock. The door soon opened, and Sergei was drawn into the house by one of the pastors. The house was completely dark, and though it took some time for his eyes to adjust to the darkness, Sergei soon could make out the faint forms of his fellow colleagues. There were fourteen of them. They greeted him warmly in hushed tones, and since Sergei was the last to arrive, they all bowed their heads in prayer to begin the meeting.

For quite some time they shared reports about the latest efforts in evangelism, and the needs that they should be most aware of. Churches and small companies of believers were springing up everywhere. The Lord was working in a mighty way to bring the gospel to the people of Moldova. People were hungry for the Word of God, and even though the government forbade any type of open evangelism, they couldn't control the longing for God in the hearts of the Moldovan people.

After this discussion the main order of business for the evening was put on the table—who would become the next conference president of the church in Moldova. A list of potential candidates was discussed, and many questions were asked about each man. Were these men godly? Did they possess the wisdom to lead God's Seventh-day Adventist people during times of persecution? Was each man's wife and family standing fully and completely behind him?

Finally the discussion came down to four names, and the one who was receiving the most attention was sitting in the room with them. His name was Victor Petya, and he had an excellent reputation in the local churches and among the conference leaders. Pastor Petya also had years of experience as an evangelist and a publisher.

For years he had worked translating the Bible and other inspirational books into the language of the Moldovan people. He had enlisted the help of women in the local churches to do the typing. At one time he had had as many as four typists working around the clock to turn out books for printing. To make multiple copies, they would insert two or three pieces of carbon paper between sheets of paper in the typewriter.

And then, through an amazing turn of events, Pastor Petya had managed to acquire a small hand press on which he could duplicate the Bibles and books. After the books were ready, Adventist leaders smuggled them out to various towns and cities where people needed them.

Some were sold secretly door-to-door by Christian book salesmen. Others were used for missionary work in cities where pastors were holding secret evangelistic meetings in the network of underground churches.

But one of the most interesting ways of distributing books and Bibles was through regular church members. This is how it worked. One of Pastor Petya's books would be carried to church on Sabbath by a deacon or elder, and then left on the floor under the church pew. Then, at some point, perhaps that Sabbath or the next, anyone who needed a book or Bible could look under the pew and take the book home for himself if he needed it. In this way the place where the book had been printed remained a secret, as well as the identity of the one who had left the book. If anyone ever was caught with the book in his home or in his hands on the street, he could honestly say, *I don't know where the book came from originally, or who printed it.*

And so, Pastor Petya's name kept coming up as a man with leadership experience, a love for the gospel, and an undying devotion for his church.

After several hours of deliberation, the men were finally ready to vote. Small slips of paper were passed out among them, and each was told to write down the name of the man he thought was most qualified for the job as president. The papers were then collected and taken to an inner room in the house where the votes were counted by candlelight.

And so it was that Pastor Victor Petya was unanimously elected that night as the new conference president. The men congratulated Pastor Petya on his new assignment. Then they bowed their heads in prayer and asked God to bless him as their new leader. Finally they all left the house and went their separate ways.

Sergei returned home by a different route than he had come. When he arrived home, Lena was already sleeping, so he slipped into bed without waking her. A cool breeze rustled the curtains hanging in the open bedroom window. Sergei could hear the late-night crickets still merrily chirping their screechy songs, and somewhere down the street a lone dog was barking.

He settled down onto his soft pillow and contemplated the previous few hours, relieved that the important meeting was finally over and that the secret police had once again been fooled as to where the conference leaders were holding a meeting. It had been a good evening.

But if Sergei thought everything was under control, he was sadly mistaken and in for a shock. He had drifted into a pleasant sleep, when suddenly there was an unexpected and violent pounding on the front door of his home.

CHAPTER 3

At first Sergei's groggy mind could not grasp what was happening, but the pounding continued. Was he dreaming? Was it his imagination working overtime, even at this late hour when the whole world should be sleeping? Was there someone at the door? He struggled to wake himself from the deep slumber into which he had fallen, but finally, through the cobwebs of sleep he began to realize that there was indeed someone at the door.

And then suddenly Lena was sitting up in bed and shaking him wide-awake. "The secret police!" she whispered hoarsely. "It's got to be the secret police!"

In the next instant Sergei leaped out of bed to answer the incessant pounding. When he opened the door, several burly policemen in uniform roughly pushed their way inside.

"Gentlemen!" Sergei fumbled for the light switch. "What's this all about?" Though he was wide awake, everything seemed like a dream as he squinted at the light now flooding the room.

A stocky, sophisticated-looking man dressed in a dark blue suit entered the house close behind the police. The man's jaw was square cut, his mustache distinguished looking, and he had on an expensive looking hat. He took one quick glance around the room, and then turned to Sergei.

"We have come to take you to headquarters!" he announced briskly. "Let's go!"

"Why? What have I done?" Sergei looked at the officer in confusion. "What am I being charged with?"

"Conducting an illegal meeting during nighttime hours, and attempting to conceal it." In spite of the man's gruff manner, Sergei could tell he felt guilty for disturbing them at such an hour.

"Do you have proof of these charges?"

"The KGB needs no proof," the officer glanced around the room again, no longer bothering to look directly at Sergei. "We only need suspicion of such actions. Put on your clothes!" he ordered impatiently. "We must be going."

Sergei knew that the charges were serious. Conducting secret meetings was considered an act of treason, punishable by beatings, prison, and on rare occasions, even execution. Sergei sent up a prayer. Help me be strong, Lord. I knew that someday they might come for me, and now it looks like they finally have.

His mind raced like lightning as he contemplated his next move. Would they even let him take anything with him? He didn't know. Should he take clothes? Would he need food? Or books? And how long would he be staying? He didn't know. The truth was, he didn't know anything.

"Shall I take a few things in a bag?" Sergei asked. He was thinking clearly now, but if he had any illusions about generosity on the part of the KGB, he was in for a rude awakening.

"There's no time for that now!" The KGB officer was emphatic. "We must go immediately!"

Sergei turned to see Lena standing behind him in the hallway; she was trembling. He wanted to tell her that everything was going to be alright, that there was nothing to worry about, but he knew it wasn't true. There was plenty to be concerned about. The KGB didn't come barging into someone's home at such an unearthly hour unless they had good reason.

"It'll be alright, dear," Sergei replied. "Everything is in God's hands." He turned to the KGB officer.

"I'd like to say goodbye to my wife, sir. Will you allow me that much?"

The KGB officer simply nodded his head in the direction of Lena.

What Sergei said during the next few moments, he would probably never remember, but Lena certainly would. "God is good, Lena." Sergei took her in his arms. "Jesus has been watching over us and holding us in the palm of His hand since the day we were born. He won't abandon us now."

He smiled bravely, but inside he was quaking. Where were these men going to take him, and what were they going to do to him?

"If I don't see you for a while, Lena, please try to be brave. God will be with you—He will be with both of us." Sergei swallowed hard. "I want you to write to your brother and see if you can go stay with him and his family for awhile. You and he are close, and I don't want you to have to be alone." Sergei glanced at the KGB officer and then at Lena again. He led her to a chair where she sat down, covered her face with her hands, and began to cry softly.

"Lena, listen to me." Sergei's voice was gentle but serious, and something in it made Lena lift her face for a moment to stop crying. "I don't know what's going to happen to me. Jesus told us long ago that if we serve Him we might have to suffer for the sake of the gospel." He shook his head slowly. "Well, now we are definitely suffering for Christ, but that's okay," he assured her. "And if we..." He stopped and tried again to say what was on his heart. "If we should not see each other again on this earth, I'll be looking for you in heaven."

Lena's eyes widened in fear, and Sergei pulled her close to him to stifle a fresh batch of tears.

"Let's go," the KGB officer ordered as he stepped toward Sergei. "We've wasted enough time."

Lena clutched at Sergei's arm, but one of the guards pulled him free. "Please be brave," Sergei reminded her. "God will take care of us. He wouldn't ask us to suffer for Him if He didn't think we could bear it."

Sergei looked at his wife tenderly. "I love you, dear. Remember, all things work together for good for those who are called to be a part of God's plan."

And then he was gone.

CHAPTER 4

At the KGB headquarters Sergei was immediately taken to an interrogation room. He sat waiting for more than an hour before the KGB officer who had arrested him finally came in. With him was a second officer, a man with cold blue eyes in an angry face. He was taller than the arresting officer, had an angular frame, and was dressed in some kind of a military uniform. And he was a chain-smoker. Sergei marveled at the way he lit up one cigarette after another like he was on some kind of a smoking marathon.

And then the questions began in rapid succession. "Where did you hold your secret meeting? We know you had a secret church meeting during the last 24 hours. What time, exactly? Who was at the meeting? Who is the next president of your organization?"

For three hours the KGB officers questioned Sergei, but always he gave them the same answer, "I can't reveal that information, gentlemen. It wouldn't be right. My church members are like family."

The mustached officer in the blue suit became impatient now, and he nodded at the other officer who was still chain-smoking cigarettes.

He leaned down close to Sergei's face, a cigarette dangling from his mouth. "If you don't give us the answers we want," he growled, "we'll use other forms of persuasion!"

Sergei knew the man was serious. KGB officers were known for their brutality. He was surprised that it had taken them this long to get physical.

The two officers left, and then a soldier came in and led Sergei away. He took Sergei to a nearby warehouse, tied him to a utility pole, and began to beat him with a rubber hose.

Sergei closed his eyes and breathed a prayer. "Please be with me, Lord." He could hear the rubber hose whistling through the air before it hit him, but to his surprise it didn't really hurt that much. In fact, he hardly felt it. How could that be, he wondered? He had been whipped before by the KGB, and it had always been a frightening experience.

But then Sergei remembered a story he had read in a book titled *The Great Controversy*. It was a story about John Wesley who was a great reformer of the church in England during the 1700s. A mob roaming the streets didn't like his preaching and was trying to run him out of town. They began to beat him using bricks and sticks and bare fists. Wesley felt the blood running down his head and face, but everything the mob did seemed to have no effect on him. In fact, he felt no pain.

Sergei had to admit that his own situation was very much like John Wesley's. He could feel the rubber hose cutting through his shirt and the welts rising, but strangely enough, he felt no pain. *Why, Lord?* he kept asking. *Why spare me? You didn't spare Jesus?*

Finally, the soldier took him back to the interrogation room. The wee hours of the morning had arrived, and Sergei knew he should be tired, but he wasn't. It was like he had his second wind, and nothing could get him down.

Sergei breathed a prayer for strength as he waited for what would come next. He asked God to be with him through this ordeal and help him to be faithful. Don't let me fail you, Father. *Don't let me waver in my resolve to honor You. You sent Your Son to live and die for me. The least I can do for You, Lord, is to suffer for the sake of the gospel. I'll do it gladly with all my soul and strength and mind.*

And then he prayed earnestly that God would help Lena to be brave. *I know she's afraid, Father, but she can be strong too.* He almost smiled to himself as he remembered her stubborn streak. She was persistent, not easily persuaded against her will, and she came by it naturally. Her father and mother were of Jewish decent and had been through severe persecution and exile at the turn of the century.

She'll make it, Sergei thought. *She's a strong woman, and I know God will help her remember the family stock from which she came.*

After another hour the two KGB officers came back and offered Sergei coffee and Russian black bread. Sergei accepted the bread but declined the coffee. As he munched on the bread, he thought of all the Bible heroes who had been persecuted because they stood for what was right—Joseph, Jeremiah, Daniel, Peter, Paul, and of course Jesus. It stirred Sergei's heart to think of their courage and faith under fire. And it made him want to be even more faithful to God in the midst of trials and persecution.

After Sergei had finished his bread, the two officers began asking questions again. Relentlessly they interrogated him, threatened him, and jumped to their feet and screamed in his face, but he wouldn't budge. It was obvious that Sergei wasn't going to betray his church members.

Finally the mustached KGB officer said, "We're finished here. We have orders to make you talk, but if you'll not talk, then there is nothing else we can do but give you the maximum penalty for criminals of your sort."

He turned to his fellow KGB officer and nodded again. The tall officer stepped closer to Sergei's chair and looked down into the preacher's face. His cold gray eyes appeared lifeless as he grimly announced, "You are now a candidate for prison in the city of Briceni! They know how to deal with your kind there!"

Sergei swallowed hard. So he was a criminal now? A criminal? For attending a secret, late-night church meeting? If this was the worst thing the KGB had to deal with on a daily basis, then they must truly have an easy life, he reasoned. But of course that didn't help him any now. No matter the crime, it appeared that the KGB were going to make Sergei pay, and dearly.

Sergei felt no resentment and no anger in his heart toward the men. It was as if the Holy Spirit had come down upon him and given him absolute peace.

But by now he was beginning to feel the effects of staying up all night. Another guard finally came and took Sergei down a long corridor and into a prison cell. The narrow cot looked so inviting that he lay down and immediately fell into an exhausted sleep. How long he slept, he didn't know, but when he awoke a guard was bringing a tin plate of food into his cell.

Sergei still had his pocket watch and pulled it out to find it was already late afternoon. He ate the borsch and black bread on his plate, and then asked the guard if he was allowed to write a letter to his wife. When the guard brought some paper and a pencil, Sergei wrote several pages and then bowed his head in prayer.

He was willing to endure any hardship for God, but he felt badly that Lena had to suffer too. But then he realized that he and his wife were in this thing together, not because he was a pastor, but because they were a team for life. They had promised to stay with one another through good times and bad, in sickness and health, 'til death should separate them. Sergei didn't know if he would ever see Lena again, or if possibly death might soon separate them, but he guessed that this should not be the most important question on their minds. More importantly, would they be faithful to God no matter what?

Sergei sat on the edge of his cot and thought about all that had happened in the last 24 hours. He had been arrested by the KGB and put through the worst of interrogations. But now, after all that had happened, something else suddenly came to mind.

Were the other pastors safe? Sergei couldn't ask anyone—if he did, the KGB might go after them too, and that would be a disaster. Fourteen other men might then be arrested, and that would be tragic for the church.

CHAPTER 5

Sergei lay back down on his cot, put his hands behind his head, and looked up at the ceiling. The biggest question in his mind now was, how had the KGB known that there was a meeting? Someone had evidently heard enough to make the connection. They had to! How else would the KGB officer have known enough to come to Sergei's house to arrest him? But then again, who could say. As the KGB officer had said, they didn't need proof—only suspicion of such actions, and a good excuse to arrest an Adventist preacher.

Sergei had been detained all night. He had been through all the usual interrogation procedures he had ever heard of—persistent questioning, shouting and screaming in the face of the victim, bright lights, and threats that intimidated him psychologically. And of course the beatings.

Sergei had to be honest with himself. He had expected such treatment by the KGB. As a witness for Jesus, he couldn't even really say he had been unjustly treated. Not if he chose to accept Jesus' challenge that Christians who preached the name of Jesus would suffer for the sake of the gospel.

And he had broken the law, after all. The laws of the land said that people were not to meet in secret meetings under cover of darkness. Sergei and his fellow pastors had tried to conceal the meeting, and from that standpoint, they had done it illegally. They were guilty, and now Sergei was paying the price.

But the laws of the land could not compete with the law of God. Sergei knew he could not allow the intimidation tactics of the KGB to interfere with God's gospel commission to the world. Jesus had asked Sergei to do his part in spreading the message of salvation to Moldova, and Sergei had accepted the challenge no matter what the price.

If Jesus suffered for crimes He never committed, then Sergei guessed he could do the same. The Son of God was humiliated and beaten and then executed. Why should a mere pastor in the heart of Moldova be surprised if God asked him to do the same.

As Sergei lay on his cot in the prison cell, he remembered the words from a passage he had memorized long ago. "Christ was treated as we deserve, that we might be treated as He deserves. He was condemned for our sins, in which He had no share, that we might be justified by His righteousness, in which we had no share. He suffered the death, which was ours, that we might receive the life, which was His. With His stripes we are healed."

More than ever before, these inspiring words helped Sergei put Jesus' great sacrifice into perspective. These words made him want to go the extra mile and endure any possible hardship for Jesus—his prayer was that he might be worthy to suffer for Jesus' sake.

But Lena's safety also weighed heavily on Sergei's mind. He only hoped that she would not have to endure hardships beyond her strength. This was his heart cry to God as he lay on the hard cot in his prison cell. His mind now shifted to his destined fate.

Briceni. The KGB were sending him to an infamous maximum-security prison in Briceni, which was known for its prisoners—men who had notorious reputations for lives of crime. To be imprisoned in Briceni would be an experience indeed! That was the understatement of the year! Would he live in fear daily? Would his life be in danger? He could hardly imagine it otherwise. Time would tell, but for now he knew he had to just wait and trust God to take care of everything.

As Sergei contemplated his fate, the scenes of his home flashed before his mind. He remembered the little kitchen and the front room with his overstuffed chair in which he loved to read. In his mind's eye he could see the end table where he always laid his Bible and the other books used in preparing his sermons. His sermon notes were probably still there, sitting on his open Bible. Lena would pack them all up for safe keeping before she left to stay with her brother. Would he ever be able to preach again?

"I guess the sermon will have to wait," Sergei sighed ironically as he stretched out on the cot and closed his eyes. For now he had bigger and more important sermons to give. His own sermon in shoes was about to begin, and he knew that it would be far more vivid than any sermon of words he might give from the pulpit. And far more effective. God would see to that, he was sure.

The next morning Sergei was put on a slow-moving train to Briceni. The northern city was less than 200 kilometers from Cahul, but the train was stopping frequently to pick up and drop off passengers along the way.

For the better part of a day, Sergei rode the train with another prisoner. The two of them were handcuffed and given only one scant meal of bread and water at noon. Sergei smiled at the simple meal. He remembered the promises in the Bible that assured him his bread and water would be sure. *You're keeping Your promise,* he reminded God with a wry sense of humor.

Sergei glanced out the window from time to time, watching the peach and plum orchards pass by. The southern region of Moldova was known for its vineyards, and they made for a very picturesque landscape from the train window. He could hardly believe that a picture of such serenity could be his on a morning when he was on his way to prison. Time and again he found himself bowing his head and praying that God would sustain him through the coming trials.

Other passengers traveling to various destinations occupied the same train car with Sergei. Although two guards had been assigned to transport the prisoners, they were pretty lenient and allowed the prisoners to get up and stretch their legs now and then. By mid-morning Sergei was visiting with the passengers sitting next to him on the train car.

Some eyed him suspiciously. With handcuffs on, they figured he had to be some kind of a criminal. But Sergei was a likable man and not easily discouraged by such conditions. And he was not one for self-pity, even under the circumstances. He leaned toward one of the passengers and said, with a twinkle in his eye, "I've been asked to go to Briceni to represent the God of heaven. The government has chosen me for the job because they know I'm a man of principle."

People were listening, but they were also watching the guards warily. If Sergei was a prisoner, why was he being so pleasant? Why was he talking about God so cheerfully? On the other hand, if he really was a criminal of some kind, they wouldn't want to show too much interest in him or be thought of as sympathizers.

The guards seemed almost indifferent to Sergei and his ability to entertain the passengers, and they finally headed out the back door of the train car for a smoke. At that point, people really began sitting up and taking notice. "What do you do for a living?" a man about his age asked him.

"I'm a pastor," Sergei said quietly. "God called me to preach the gospel of Jesus in my hometown. The good news of the gospel is that Jesus, God's Son, came to die for us and save us from sin, because we are His children." The train car was deathly quiet now, and all eyes were on him. Sergei realized he was being given a chance for a mini Bible study, and he wasn't about to lose the opportunity. He might be on his way to prison, but he was going to share the gospel as surely as if he were in his pulpit back home.

CHAPTER 6

The click-clack of the train wheels on the track punctuated Sergei's comments. "Today, Jesus is in heaven preparing a home for everyone who chooses to believe in the Son of God." He glanced toward heaven. "Some day soon Jesus will come back in the clouds of heaven to take us to live with Him in heaven. This will bring an end to sin and sickness and sorrow as we know it today."

"You look like such a nice young man," a little babushka with a quavering voice half whispered. "So, why the handcuffs?"

"I am a servant of God," Sergei smiled. "The government tried to force me to provide information about my fellow church leaders, but they are like family to me. I refused to betray their trust."

By now the guards were back, and they were beginning to take notice. This man was receiving more attention from the passengers than they would have expected for a government prisoner. Sergei spoke for a few more minutes on the love of Jesus, but finally one of the guards, pointed at him. "Stop!" the guard shouted, obviously annoyed with Sergei. "Come with me!" he ordered, leading the way down the aisle of the train car and out the door at the back. Sergei knew now that the chance to witness for his faith had ended, but he thanked God he had been able to introduce a carload of passengers to Jesus.

They walked through several more train cars until the guard finally opened the door to the baggage car. "You can stay here for the rest of the trip," he growled. He nodded over his shoulder as the second guard entered the car behind them. "Mikhail, here, will keep you company!" he sneered.

Sergei sat down on the cold metal floor, leaned against the wall, and closed his eyes. This was a clear case of solitary confinement, intended to isolate him from the other passengers. The devil had interrupted his Bible study and his chance to speak for God on the train, and now the window of opportunity had closed.

But God wasn't through with Sergei yet.

Mikhail pulled a cigarette from his coat pocket and lit it. As he puffed on the cigarette, he watched Sergei. Finally, he sat down beside him on the floor.

"So you're a preacher, are you?" he continued puffing on the cigarette. "I used to go to Sunday Mass when I was a boy."

"Really," Sergei was interested now.

"My mother and father used to take me to a Greek Orthodox Church. Those were good days," he mused. "We lived in Straseni, and my parents were very religious. In spite of what the government said about the superiority of communism, my father always said God was the only real answer to the problems of a country."

Mikhail dropped the finished butt of his cigarette on the floor and smudged it out with his foot. "My father didn't have a formal education. Not much beyond basic preparatory school, anyway. He left after his ninth year of school, but he liked to read. He became a self-educated man, and he learned a lot about Soviet history and politics. My mother says she thinks he talked too much, because one day the KGB came and took him away. We never saw him again." Mikhail's face was bitter. "I was only seven."

"I'm sorry," was all Sergei could say. "I'm very sorry."

"No matter!" Mikhail retorted indignantly. "I've never had much use for God since then! My father was a religious man, and God couldn't even protect him against his own government!"

"And joining the Communist Red Army? It hasn't helped much either, has it?" Sergei glanced at the uniformed guard.

"I guess you could say that." Mikhail took off his green military cap.

"But?" Sergei studied Mikhail's stern face.

Mikhail eyed Sergei curiously. "You are very perceptive," he began to chuckle. "I know! I know! You're going to say there are no buts when it comes to God. Huh! That sounds just like my father."

"And you still believe that too, don't you?"

"Maybe?" Mikhail began turning his cap round and round in his hand.

"Your father was a wise man," Sergei said. "He didn't die for nothing, you know?"

"That's what my mother always said. If it was worth believing, she said it was worth living for—and dying for."

"I've always thought so," Sergei nodded, "and when it comes to standing up for God, it's doubly so."

Mikhail squinted in Sergei's direction. "I believe you really mean that. How does that work for you?"

"It's simple. Jesus came to this world and stood up against the religious leaders of the day. He never backed down, and in the end they crucified Him on a cruel cross." Sergei's voice was solemn. "Jesus was not afraid to do this for me! How can I do less for Him? I'll get my reward soon, when He comes again to take me home to heaven. For now, I'm content to represent Him here and tell as many people as possible about the good news of the gospel."

"Wow!" Mikhail hung his head again in respect. "You sound so sure of yourself."

"I am, and you can be too, Mikhail. Just believe it! This is your chance to be sure of your salvation. Why not do it here, today? We can pray about it now if you want?"

And so they prayed after their heartfelt discussion, and Mikhail gave his heart to Jesus. It was all so moving for Sergei that he didn't know how long they had been riding or how far they had come. Only as he felt the train start to slow and the breaks begin to squeal, did he realize the trip was nearly over.

The next stage in his ordeal was about to begin. What would it be like in the government prison? What would they put him through? Would he have to suffer much? Would he remain faithful to God?

There was no doubt in Sergei's mind that by God's strength he would make it, and through it all he would continue to be a brave witness for God. He had to. How could he do anything else? After all, Jesus had suffered so much for him.

CHAPTER 7

Late that afternoon Sergei arrived at the government prison in Briceni and was turned over to the warden. He was discouraged as he saw the thick stone walls of the prison. There were high barbed wire fences surrounding the prison too, just in case someone tried to escape.

When the warden heard the charges brought against Sergei, he stepped out from behind his office desk and scowled at Sergei nose-to-nose. His hulking frame towered over Sergei, and his steel-gray crew-cut hair gave him the look of a tough marine sergeant. "So! They've brought you to me!" he crowed. "I'm sure you've heard of the prison here at Briceni! My reputation as a warden precedes me, I trust."

Sergei only nodded politely. What could he say?

"Have you anything to say in your defense?" the warden barked, his beady black eyes boring holes through Sergei.

Sergei hesitated only a moment. Not daring to look the warden in the eye, he said, "I'm here because I'm a Christian pastor. If that makes me a criminal, then I'm guilty."

"Don't get smart with me!" snapped the warden, his face as hard as though it were chiseled in stone. "That's exactly what you are! A criminal, and don't you forget it!"

"I intend to make an example of you!" he continued. "What you're going to get is solitary confinement for a while! We'll see if that knocks some sense into you!" he growled, baring his teeth. "If you have to go hungry for awhile, maybe that will help straighten out your thinking. Maybe that will teach you not to disobey the orders of a government official!"

Two guards accompanied them as the warden led the way to a row of small concrete cells on the first level of the prison complex. "Well now, here we are, preacher! I'm sure you will find the quarters to your liking! Nice and lonely! Ha! Ha! Ha!" he scoffed, his face full of hatred. Sergei couldn't ever remember having seen anyone more angry and bitter.

The warden gave Sergei a push into the cell. "You can have all the time you want to spend with your God in there! Ha! Ha!" he laughed again. "On the other hand, if you are willing to get rid of these foolish notions about your God, we might be able to arrange for some nice Russian bread. Eh! What do you say to that?" The warden roared with laughter as he clanged the iron door shut.

Sergei bowed his head quietly. No food! Nothing to eat! How long could he last without food! He had fasted for two or three days at a time before, but this would be nothing like that! He didn't know what exactly he had expected. A beating, maybe, or some more interrogations, but no food! Without food, how could he stay warm in this cold weather?

"I said, what do you say to that!" the warden demanded again, as he stared at Sergei through the tiny window of the cell door.

Sergei hesitated. What could he say to this evil man? The warden had it in his power to do whatever he wanted with Sergei. He could starve him, beat him, even kill him if he wanted, and there was nothing anyone could do about it!

"Scared, eh? Coming to your senses, are you!" The warden snorted and started to turn away. "Well, that's good! This business of God has got to go! There is no God, and you know it as well as I do!"

"No!" Sergei called to the warden suddenly. He knew he had to say something. "There is a God!" his eyes flashed in righteous indignation. "He is my Defender, and I must be faithful to Him. His Son Jesus died for my sins so I could have eternal life. I can't do less for Him than He has done for me." Sergei was looking the warden dead in the eye now through the small window in the cell door, and his nerve took the warden by surprise.

"I can't turn my back on Jesus!" Sergei added. "My God can supply all my needs through His Son Jesus! He can, but even if He doesn't, I will still remain faithful to Him, so help me God!"

"Supply your every need! Huh!" the warden had regained his composure by now. "Listen to me!" he snarled, his face contorted with rage. "I'm telling you, there is no God! What's wrong with you Christians! Are you insane!" He made a fist and shook it at Sergei angrily. "You know what, preacher! You're a dead man!" he growled, glaring at Sergei. "Starting right now you'll get no bread from me! Only water! I swear I'll let you starve before I feed you again! If your God is so strong, let Him bring you bread Himself!"

The warden pointed at Sergei, a fiendish look in his eye. "I'll come back another time when you're willing to talk some sense! No one in their right mind behaves like this!" He turned and walked away, calling over his shoulder. "We'll see what your God does for you now!"

Sergei watched the warden go before glancing around his prison cell. There was very little in it. Only a bed with a very thin mattress and blanket on it, a wooden chair, and a chamber pot since there was no bathroom.

Above his bed was a small window with bars across it. He could feel an early evening wind blowing in through the window, but he couldn't see out through it. The window was big enough to let in a little light, but too small to crawl through even if he could break the bars out. He knew he could not hope to escape. And if he did escape from the prison, where would he go? The guards would find him and catch him for sure. He knew they wouldn't be sympathetic toward a man who was religious. The military taught its men that religion was for pathetic, weak-minded souls.

Sergei peered out through the small window in his cell door again. The guards could look in on him now and then, and Sergei could look out to see what was going on in the prison yard. It looked like the prisoners were allowed out of their cells to exercise a little, but Sergei doubted he was going to get a chance to do any time soon. It looked like solitary confinement was the name of the game in this prison when someone was to be punished.

The sun went down on Sergei in that lonely little prison cell. As the dusk faded into the cold of darkness, the hours passed slowly. It was early spring, so the stone floors and walls made the prison cell feel even chillier. Sergei knelt down and prayed. He knew he needed to be courageous and strong for God. This was not the first time he had been imprisoned for his faith, but he didn't remember ever feeling so lonely and forsaken.

"Oh, God of my fathers!" Sergei prayed. "I need you now more than ever. Persecution can be a hard thing, Lord, and I don't know how bad things will get before they get better! You have not failed me in the past, Lord! My faith may be weak, but You are strong. Please help me to be faithful to You here in this prison now."

Once again Sergei thought of Lena. What was she doing right now? How was she holding up? Was she continuing to lead out in the worship services at their church? Was she feeling as lonely and afraid as he was? Sergei knew he was just going to have to trust God to care for her while he was here in this prison, however long that might be.

179

"Please, Lord," he prayed, "let my suffering be worth all the risk Lena and I have taken for You and the church back home."

Sergei lay down on his bed for the night. He shivered in his thin coat. The moth-eaten blanket made little difference in the cold night air that drifted through the open windows. And his stomach growled like a hungry animal. With nothing in him to give him energy, he knew it was going to be a long, cold night.

"My God will supply all my needs through Christ Jesus!" Sergei reminded himself courageously.

CHAPTER 8

Early the next morning before Sergei had even opened his eyes he heard a strange sound, as if something were scratching on the window ledge above his bed. He sat up to listen and turned to see what was making the noise, but the window was too high up. Finally he stood on his bed, reached up to the ledge, and felt around until his hand rested on something soft. It felt like a piece of bread, but he knew it couldn't be! What would a piece of bread be doing on the window ledge?

He pulled it down to examine it, and to his astonishment, it was indeed bread. Russian black bread. "What is this?" Sergei couldn't believe his eyes. "Is this possible, Lord! You have sent someone to bring me bread to eat already? It's Russian bread like my Lena makes for me every day back home!"

But how did it get there, Sergei wondered. Had a sympathetic guard heard the conversation Sergei had had with the warden? Had the guard felt sorry for him and brought the bread to him in secret? Sergei could only guess.

He got down off the bed and knelt to thank God in gratefulness. He hadn't eaten anything since noon the day before, but the Lord had provided food for him, and now he could eat. "Lord, You are so good to me! Your power knows no limits! I was so foolish, Lord, and so weak to doubt You! Thank you for this wonderful gift!"

After blessing his meager meal, Sergei sat down on his bed to enjoy the bread. It might be only one slice, but it was food, and it seemed like a meal fit for a king. And then suddenly it occurred to him that if he ate the bread, the warden would never see proof of Sergei's good fortune. The warden would never know that God had indeed provided food for Sergei.

I've just got to use this opportunity to tell the warden what my God has done for me! Sergei pondered his next move. *If the warden should ask me whether my God has provided for my every need, I want to be able to show him the proof.* He clutched at his empty stomach, which was growing louder than ever. *But I'm so hungry. I haven't eaten since yesterday when that guard on the train tossed me a crust of bread!*

Sergei didn't know what to do. He remembered the Bible promise he had recited to himself the night before about his bread and water being sure. Well, his bread and water were here now, but without a little self control on Sergei's part, the warden would never see the proof. Not if Sergei ate it, anyway.

"Oh, no, no!" Sergei groaned aloud to himself at the thought. He didn't want to think about fasting longer. But the more he thought about it, the more he knew he had to do it. He had to show the warden the fulfillment of God's promise, that God could provide for his every need. For God, and the gospel, and the warden, he had no other choice. He had to do this!

Reluctantly Sergei set the bread aside. He would have to put the slice away and save it so the warden could see it when he came around to check on Sergei. But where to put it? If he put it out of sight, he wouldn't be as likely to be tempted to eat it. And then he thought of his mattress and lifted it. He could leave the bread there so the rats wouldn't get to it as easily. Sergei hadn't seen any rats around yet, but he knew there were probably a few. Lifting the straw tick mattress, he put the black bread on the wooden boards, and then laid the mattress back down.

Sergei waited patiently all morning to show the bread to the warden, but the man never came. Sometimes Sergei got the slice of bread out to look at it. He wanted to eat it, but when he thought of the look he would see on the warden's face at sight of the bread, he always put it back.

CHAPTER 9

By late afternoon Sergei was getting very hungry. It was near dusk, and Sergei was beginning to think he would just eat the slice of bread, but suddenly he heard the scratching sound again up near the window. The sound grew louder, but he couldn't see anything. Sergei got up on his bed again and felt on the window ledge, and there to his amazement was another slice of bread. He took the slice of bread down and laid it on the chair. Then he took the first slice of bread from under the mattress and laid it on the chair beside the second slice.

A feeling of almost indescribable awe came over Sergei. "I don't believe it!" he said out loud, his eyes wide again. "Well, actually, I do believe it," he grinned, "but twice? This is too good to be true! Am I dreaming, Lord?" he raised his eyes to heaven and chuckled. "You have blessed me twice, even if I haven't tasted of Your blessings yet."

Two slices of bread. It was no accident that the bread had showed up on the window ledge a second time. Sergei was sure of it. Someone out there knew of Sergei's situation and was bringing him bread. There was no other explanation.

Sergei wanted more than anything to climb up and look out the window to see where the bread might have come from, but the window was too high up. He kept looking up at the window, and he finally decided that if he turned his cot on end and climbed up on top of it, he might be able to see out the window. However, when he had climbed up high enough to look out, there was no one in sight. All he could see was a tree near the window and an open prison yard with the prison fence beyond. No one was in sight. Whoever was bringing him the bread evidently didn't want to be discovered, and Sergei could hardly blame him. If it was a guard—and it surely must be—Sergei knew he would be punished severely by the warden. Or worse. Sergei didn't want to think of that possibility.

Sergei climbed back down and set the cot and mattress back in their place. He guessed it didn't really matter how the bread had ended up on the window ledge. God had arranged for it to be there, and that was good enough for Sergei.

Sergei sat down and stared at the bread on the chair. He had two slices now—one to eat and another to hold in reserve so the warden would have proof of the miracle meals God was bringing him.

He could eat the first slice from that morning before it got too old and save the second slice for the warden to see. But first he would thank his Father in heaven for providing him bread to eat in his lonely prison cell.

He bowed his head to pray, but then stopped. If one slice of bread would surprise the warden, think what two slices would do as a witness to God's power. The thought of such a thing gave him a feeling of desperation though. He was so very hungry.

Sergei put his head in his hands and contemplated what he should do. To decide against eating the bread required so much self-control, but the more he thought about it, the more certain he was of what he should do. He must save both slices of bread. Tenderly, almost reverently, he returned the first slice of bread to its place under the mattress, laid the second one beside it, and put the mattress back down on top of the bread.

Again he hoped there were no rats around. If the rats ate the bread, how could he show it to the warden? But then, again, he guessed that if God could give him the bread in the first place, he could protect the two slices.

"Please, Lord!" Sergei prayed. "Give me strength to go through with this! Help me to be courageous and patient."

Darkness came again, and with it the cold night air. With no books to read, and no light in his cell to read by anyway, the evenings were going to be long. After another season of prayer, Sergei lay down and tried to get some sleep. But sleep wouldn't come. The coldness of the night made him shiver uncontrollably, and he clutched at the blanket all the more tightly, trying to keep warm.

The thought that he had two whole slices of bread beneath his mattress was nearly driving him crazy. He had promised himself he wouldn't eat the bread, but without it in his stomach he was having a hard time keeping warm, and for what? So the warden would have proof that God could provide for Sergei's every need? Who cared about the warden! He was just a heartless old geezer who cared little about the suffering he was putting his prisoners through! That was one way to look at it.

But then Sergei thought some more about it! Proving to the warden that God could provide for Sergei would be more like proving to him that there was a God in the first place. The warden didn't even believe in God! When Sergei thought about it that way, it suddenly seemed much more important. Not eating the two slices of bread he had stashed under his mattress was really a matter of life and death then. Not for him maybe, but certainly for the warden.

"Praise God from whom all blessings flow! Praise Him all creatures here below!" Sergei began singing to keep himself warm and to lift his spirits. "Praise Him above ye heavenly host! Praise Father, Son, and Holy Ghost!"

Sergei rubbed his growling stomach and felt a sense of peace and warmth come over him. It was amazing! How had that happened? The peace he felt seemed sensible enough. He had felt peace many times after praying to God. But the warmth he felt right now was unbelievable! Unexpected! He knew the temperature must be down near zero degrees Celsius, and yet he was warm. It was truly amazing! Miraculous was more like it! All he had on was a shirt and a light coat. The thin blanket should be making little difference, and yet he was still unexplainably warm.

"Thank you, Lord!" he whispered. "You've done it again! Amazing! Truly amazing!" And with that he drifted off to sleep.

CHAPTER 10

Sergei's eyes opened suddenly. It was morning again and something had awakened him. The faint streaks of dawn were already sending their pink fingers in through the metal bars of his cell window. In spite of the cold, he felt rested this morning, as though he had slept a full night at home in his own bed.

He lay there for a few moments remembering how warm he had felt when he went to sleep the night before. It had given him a wonderful feeling of peace, and he still felt that warmth now. And then he remembered the two slices of bread under his mattress. He hoped the warden would come to his cell soon and see the slices of bread, then this whole thing would be over and he could eat the bread. Or maybe the warden would see that it was pointless to deprive Sergei of food any longer and let him eat his meals along with the rest of the prisoners.

Sergei slid out of bed and onto his knees. The crisp morning air made the floor even colder, but he ignored the feeling. *Thank you, Lord, for every good thing in life,* he prayed.

And then almost as if on queue, he heard a sound and glanced up at the window. Had the guard returned to put another slice of bread on the ledge again? A third time would be phenomenal!

It was not yet light enough to see clearly, but Sergei thought he saw a faint shadow, and then he heard the scratching sound again. He tried to peer through the early morning darkness, but it was no use. He could see nothing.

When he climbed up on his bed and reached up on the window ledge, there was another slice of bread. He brought it down and carefully cradled it in his hands. Three slices of bread now. What a miracle, and again it looked like Lena's bread! Soft and fresh, probably made just the night before.

"I don't believe it, Lord!" Sergei breathed deeply of the bread as he held it close to his nose. "Well, actually, I do believe it! This is three times now!" He glanced up at the window again. "It seems too good to be true, Lord! Am I dreaming?" he chuckled to himself. "You have blessed me three times now."

Sergei bowed his head in gratefulness, and a sense of relief flooded over him. He could finally eat a piece of bread now. He had two slices of bread under his mattress and another in his hands. Two slices to prove to the warden that God had been watching over him. Sergei would show the warden that he served a real God who could provide real food for His children.

He laid the new piece of bread on the chair, and then took out the other two slices from beneath the mattress. Three slices! It was a wonderfully glorious sight!

But something within him wouldn't allow him to eat any of it! Something about the whole situation seemed unresolved. He stared at the three slices on the chair. Was the warden never going to come back! Sergei wasn't going to starve, at least not as long as the guard—or whoever it might be—was bringing him bread.

Sergei thought about the warden long and hard. He was obviously a bitter, angry man. Sergei thought he knew what it was the warden wanted from this situation, but did he? Was it that the warden hated Christian pastors this much? Was the warden sadistic, taking delight in starving Sergei, or was it something else? Did the warden have something to prove? When he had talked with Sergei two days before, he seemed pretty determined to prove that there wasn't a God. "There is no God!" he had shouted. "This business of God has got to go!"

Sergei set his jaw and got a strange look in his eye. The warden wanted more than anything to prove to Sergei that there was no God—or maybe the warden was trying to prove it to himself. Sergei closed his eyes and thought about that. The man must have had some bad experiences.

Well, Sergei wasn't going to help the warden keep that idea going any longer than he had to. The warden wanted to prove that God was dead, or didn't exist at all, but Sergei was determined to prove that God was very much alive. He wanted the warden to know that God cared enough for a Moldovan pastor to see to it that he had bread every day in a lonely government prison cell.

By now Sergei knew what he must do. The warden would come to see how Sergei was doing sooner or later, and if one or two slices of bread would seem like a miracle from God, then three slices would be even better. It was a tortuous decision, but he knew he had to do it. He lifted the mattress and laid the three slices side by side on the boards of his bed. Then he quickly laid the mattress down before he could change his mind.

As Sergei sat down on the edge of his bed, he thought about the story in the Bible when Elijah was fed by ravens. It was an amazing story, and he wondered, *Is it possible that God is feeding me with ravens here in this prison cell?* He hadn't heard any cawing or flapping of wings, but the shadow in the early morning light had been a dark one. The more he thought about it, the more excited he became. And if the bread had been sent three times, how many more times would it come?

The day dragged on, and that evening another slice of bread miraculously appeared on the window ledge. And the next morning another one arrived. In fact, for three days, morning and evening, the slices arrived, and every time Sergei would stash them away, until there were six slices of black Russian bread lined up under his mattress. Sometimes he heard the bread being placed on the window ledge, and sometimes he didn't, but always it was there at dawn and dusk.

By now Sergei's resolve had been built up. He would wait for the warden to come, no matter what it took, and then the warden would see just how much God had provided for him. He was terribly hungry, but he was tough, too. He had fasted before with church members when praying for special concerns in the church. And he had been in prison before, so he knew what real hunger felt like. It could be excruciating, but right now it felt pretty splendid knowing that the Lord was working in a mighty way. Though Sergei was terribly hungry, each slice of bread that was added to the others under his mattress was a testimony to God's power. It was proof that God exists, and that He could and would provide for those who were dependent on Him. Each time Sergei thought of this, he drew strength from it and felt sure that in the end he would have the last word after all.

"If I live to tell about it!" Sergei would joke to himself. "The warden's trying to starve me to death, and meanwhile I'm refusing to eat the evidence that's been under my mattress all along!" He smiled as he sat on the edge of his bed, "But even if I die, the warden will still see the bread. He'll have to. When he cleans out my cell, he'll find the evidence right here under my mattress."

187

Sergei looked heavenward. "Lord, you went 40 days without food, so I suppose I can wait a few days, too. But please hurry, Lord! I don't want to spoil Your plan! I don't want to get weak and give in to my hunger!"

CHAPTER 11

It was the morning of Sergei's fifth day in the Soviet prison at Briceni. The night had been chilly as usual, but Sergei had slept well again. He couldn't explain why he was resting so well. In spite of the cold temperatures in his prison cell, with only a shirt and light coat on, he still felt warm. To Sergei it was an unexplainable miracle.

And then there were the slices of Russian black bread which was a whole string of miracles. Sergei had now received six pieces of bread from some benevolent provider, but miracle or not he felt he just couldn't eat any of them. They would provide such a wonderful chance to witness to the warden.

As he lay on his bed, waking to the horizon's pinks and ambers of another day, Sergei wondered—would there be another slice of the black bread on the window ledge this morning? The routine had established itself for three days now, but did he really need any more bread? He had enough to serve as a testimony to God's power to provide, but if the warden didn't come soon, at some point in the near future Sergei would probably need to begin eating pieces of the bread. In the cold spring air, the bread kept quite well, but it wouldn't last forever. No rats had come into Sergei's cell as of yet, but he couldn't be sure that they would stay away forever, especially at night when he was sleeping.

Sergei listened for the scratching sound above him on the window ledge, but he heard nothing. He finally rolled out of bed, slipped to his knees, and began to pray as he did this time every morning. He thanked God for a good nights sleep and for the bread he knew God would be sending.

Then a thought struck him—maybe the bread had already come. Maybe Sergei had overslept and already missed the provider this morning. But as he climbed up on his bed and reached to the window's ledge, he found nothing. Would this be the day the bread would stop coming? *Six slices are enough to show the warden, aren't they?*

Suddenly he heard footsteps, and Sergei recognized the warden's voice. A flutter of thoughts raced through Sergei's mind as he realized that the warden had finally come. He jumped to his feet, his heart racing and his hands shaking. Now he could show the warden the six slices of bread. Now the warden would see that God does indeed provide for those who trust in Him. Now he would believe in the power and very existence of God.

The warden stepped up to the little window in the cell door and peered through at Sergei. "Well preacher, has your God supplied your every need?" he sneered, his beady black eyes squinting with enjoyment.

"I can't complain," Sergei bowed his head humbly.

"Can't complain!" the warden taunted. "I bet you're hungry!"

"I'm hungry, it's true," Sergei said.

The warden looked him up and down disdainfully. "Well, I see you're none the worse for your days in solitary confinement. A bit thinner, and maybe a bit more pale, but I bet you're wiser, too, huh?"

"Much wiser, sir."

"Then you have come to your senses and decided to end this foolishness we spoke of before! This nonsense about your God—whoever that is!"

"Sir, actually I was just thanking my God this very morning for all He has given me. Life and a healthy body and—"

"But has He given you what you need most? Food?"

"Actually, sir, He has." Sergei had a twinkle in his eye.

"He has?" the warden screwed up his face in surprise.

"Yes, sir, He has! It's just that—well—I just haven't eaten any of it yet."

"Haven't eaten any of—What do you mean by that!" the warden interrupted himself, a confused look on his face.

"My God has supplied all my needs," Sergei repeated. "I just wanted you to see it."

For the first time Sergei saw a look of uncertainty cross the warden's face. He appeared as gruff as ever, but his look of scorn had turned to surprise now.

"You see, sir. He gave me bread." Sergei smiled at the warden sheepishly. The moment had come. It was time to show the warden the evidence. God had indeed provided for Sergei's every need. At least it seemed like it to Sergei. He had expected nothing more than the peace of God in his heart, and God had given him much more. He had given Sergei courage on the train to Briceni. He had given him warmth on the cold nights, and He had given him bread every morning and night. But just as importantly, God had given Sergei the willingness to witness for Jesus. He had given him the willpower to not eat the bread.

Sergei walked to his cot, lifted the mattress, and pointed to the six slices of bread. "Look here, sir. My God has supplied all my needs through His riches in Christ Jesus. My God has promised that if I'm faithful to Him, He will never fail me or forsake me, and this is living proof that He has kept His promise."

An incredible peace flooded over Sergei's soul as he stared at the warden through the tiny window in his cell door. It was as if Sergei didn't care anymore what happened to him. No matter what the warden could throw at him, Sergei was sure that God would help him get through the ordeal. God was here in this prison cell giving Sergei his every need—and much more.

It took a moment, but the warden suddenly got his bearings. "What in the world?" he sputtered. "I don't understand! Where—where did this bread come from?"

He threw the bolt lock aside, swung the door open, and came running into the cell to stare at the bread. "Where did this bread come from!" he shouted. "Who's done this? Who brought you the bread?" He grabbed Sergei by the shoulders and began to shake him. Sergei had to admit that it wasn't quite what he had been expecting. Somehow he had thought the warden would break down and apologize to Sergei, and maybe confess that there was a God in heaven after all.

"Which of the guards did this?" the warden demanded angrily. "I'll have them horse whipped!"

Sergei stared at the warden in surprise, but he knew he had to say something. "Actually, sir, I don't know who brought it. All I know is that every morning and evening I hear a scratching at the window, and when I climb up on my bed and check the window ledge, the bread is always there."

"But—but, who is doing this!" the warden roared.

Sergei shrugged at the warden. "All I can say is, I trusted the Lord, and He has supplied my need."

CHAPTER 12

For a moment the warden said nothing. He just stared at Sergei as though he believed him just a little, maybe. But only for a moment.

"Who brought you bread?" he demanded once again. "This is the last time I'm going to ask you!"

And then the inevitable happened. While the warden was fussing and fuming about who it was that might have been bringing Sergei the bread, there was a telltale scratching at the window ledge again. And then Sergei saw a shadow darken the opening in the wall above his bed. It was still barely light enough to see, but the dawn was getting brighter with every passing minute.

As of yet, Sergei had never seen his benefactor. Whoever had brought him bread obviously didn't want to be discovered. Didn't want to be caught bringing bread to a prisoner the warden had sworn he would starve.

Sergei stared up at the window. Was it indeed a guard who had been bringing him the bread? The guard would be able to climb the tree, that much was sure. Or was it someone or something else? Sergei squinted his eyes into the growing light. Was it a raven? Or might it be an angel? Angels didn't make shadows, did they? It didn't matter. Whether it was a raven or an angel, it was still a miracle.

The two men stepped backward to get a better look at who it might be.

And then suddenly, to Sergei's and the warden's surprise, there appeared on the window ledge a large black cat with a piece of bread in its mouth. Both men stood there dumbfounded, their mouths open in shocked surprise.

Sergei was the first to find his voice. "Praise God from whom all blessings flow! It was a cat! My God has supplied my every need by sending a cat!" He stared up at the cat, and then back at the warden. This was even better than he had imagined it could be!

But by the look in the warden's eye, Sergei knew that something even more incredible had happened. And he was right.

The warden rolled his eyes and kept repeating, "I do not believe my eyes. I see it, but I do not believe it! This is impossible!" His eyes were earnest now, and in place of his scowl was a look of awe and wonder. "I have never seen such a miracle," he confessed. "Your God exists, after all, and today He will be my God too."

Sergei could see that the struggle in the warden's heart was at its end. The man had come full circle and now seen the light.

"Today you have shown me what I refused to see all these years." The warden bowed his head in humble shame. "Not only has your God sent you bread morning and evening these past few days, but He has sent it to you as a gift from me! You see, preacher—this is—this is my..." He stumbled on his words and swallowed hard. "This is my daughter's cat—and—and that bread in its mouth—is—is my wife's bread from my own kitchen table!"